Learn API Testing

Norms, Practices, and Guidelines for Building Effective Test Automation

Jagdeep Jain

Apress®

Learn API Testing: Norms, Practices, and Guidelines for Building Effective Test Automation

Jagdeep Jain
Dewas, Madhya Pradesh, India

ISBN-13 (pbk): 978-1-4842-8141-3   ISBN-13 (electronic): 978-1-4842-8142-0
https://doi.org/10.1007/978-1-4842-8142-0

Managing Director, Apress Media LLC: Welmoed Spahr
Acquisitions Editor: Divya Modi
Development Editor: James Markham
Coordinating Editor: Divya Modi
Copy Editor: Mary Behr

Cover designed by eStudioCalamar

Cover image designed by Freepik (www.freepik.com)

Distributed to the book trade worldwide by Springer Science+Business Media New York, 1 New York Plaza, Suite 4600, New York, NY 10004-1562, USA. Phone 1-800-SPRINGER, fax (201) 348-4505, e-mail orders-ny@springer-sbm.com, or visit www.springeronline.com. Apress Media, LLC is a California LLC and the sole member (owner) is Springer Science + Business Media Finance Inc (SSBM Finance Inc). SSBM Finance Inc is a **Delaware** corporation.

For information on translations, please e-mail booktranslations@springernature.com; for reprint, paperback, or audio rights, please e-mail bookpermissions@springernature.com.

Apress titles may be purchased in bulk for academic, corporate, or promotional use. eBook versions and licenses are also available for most titles. For more information, reference our Print and eBook Bulk Sales web page at www.apress.com/bulk-sales.

Any source code or other supplementary material referenced by the author in this book is available to readers on GitHub via the book's product page, located at https://github.com/Apress/Learn-API-Testing.

For more detailed information, please visit https://github.com/Apress/Learn-API-Testing.

Printed on acid-free paper

*I dedicate this book to my teachers, mentors,
and colleagues who have been instrumental in
the enhancement of my knowledge on the subject,
and also to my wife, daughter, sisters, parents, and in-laws,
without whose relentless support it would not have been
possible to manage the tight schedule of this work.*

—Jagdeep Jain

Table of Contents

About the Author

Jagdeep Jain has a Bachelor of Computer Science and Engineering degree and more than 15 years of rich experience in the software quality assurance and testing domain. He has worked for several product development software companies. He is a firm believer and an avid advocate of test automation. He is also the co-author of *Pro Apache JMeter* with Sai Matam.

About the Technical Reviewers

Nitesh Kumar Jain has over a decade of experience in the software testing world. He has an M.Tech in Information Technology from IIITM Gwalior, M.P. and a B.E. in Computer Science and Engineering from NIT Raipur, Chattisgarh. He is a keen technology learner with a "let's automate everything" attitude. He is also an ISTQB-certified Test Manager, Technical Test Analyst, and Agile Test Engineer. He loves to make Java/Swing-based tools that can help with anything related to software testing. He is presently working as a Lead QA at https://watermarkinsights.com and is constantly involved in doing quality work on framework design for UI, API, and performance test automation. His LinkedIn profile is https://www.linkedin.com/in/nitesh-jain-958a2630/.

Kushagra Mittal has a Bachelor of Technology in Computer Science degree from Amity University, Lucknow, UP. He has over nine years of experience in developing back-end solutions for multinational companies and has built products that are used by thousands of customers. He has developed microservices using Java Spring Boot and has used the Swagger UI for API documentation. He has hosted various training sessions with the University of Lucknow, UP on big data, distributed systems, and machine learning. He is an Oracle-certified Java Programmer, Oracle Cloud Infrastructure Foundation Certified Associate, and AWS Certified Developer - Associate. He is currently working as a Principal Member of Technical Staff at Oracle India Pvt. Ltd. His LinkedIn profile is https://www.linkedin.com/in/kushagra-mittal/.

Acknowledgments

I want to thank everyone who helped in giving shape to this book, including but not limited to providing useful and timely feedback on the chapters, source code, and test scripts, and finding bugs in the sample web applications. Without them, it would have been tough to create *good quality work* for you, the reader.

Thanks to Nidhi Jain for reviewing each and every line of the book with *the* objective of improving readability.

Nitin Dhawan works as a program manager and he has helped various teams in setting up scrum best practices and implementing planning, monitoring, and risk assessment modules. Currently he is working as a technical program manager and is responsible for establishing the communication channel between engineering teams by ensuring regular communication on projects/programs and status to everyone. Thanks to Nitin for reviewing the case study chapter. It was a big help to get all of the angles on how the software industry works in the scrum model.

Thanks to Aashita Priya, Advocate Jayant R. Vipat, Akshay Muramatti, Amudhan Kash, Anand Sinha, Anuj Yadav, Arun Vijapur, Arijit Hawlader, Aruna Piraviperumal, Ashish Mankar, Beejal Vibhakar, Bharat Vipat, Deepika Sharma, Ganesh Phirke, Ganesh Prasath S, Gomtesh Gandhi, Gyan Bhal, Haridev Vengateri, Harshad Savot, Harshvardhan Vipat, Jay Erb, Jay Shah, Jaya Gopal Somu, Jon Gunnip, Kevendra Patidar, Laura King, Mangesh Lunawat, Marque Davis, Matt Armstrong ,Michael Laube, Monica Poddar, Mukesh Bafna, Nehal Gaikwad, Nikhil Agrawal, Nitish Shirsath, Niti Dugar, Pankaj Saraf, Patrick Lee, Peeyush Janoria,

ACKNOWLEDGMENTS

Piyush Singh, Prasad Jakka, Prasoon Kumar, Qian Li, Rajat Jain, Rangith Vaddepally, Ramanuj Vipat, Ramesh Sunkara, Rohit Bagde, Sai Matam, Sathya Gowri N, Shally Garg, Sharon Annese, Shravan Belde, Snehal Mundle, Stella Yun, Sudeep Tripathy, Tapan Upadhyay, Tarak Joshi, Tina Bajaj, Tulasi R. Meeniga, Vidhut Singh, Vijaay Doraiswamy, Vijay Santore, Yogesh Sharma, and Zhelyazko Tumbev for enriching my skill set, technical expertise, and knowledge on software development practices and principles, and for keeping me motivated each and every day.

I am very thankful to the editorial team at Apress and the technical reviewer for having various checkpoints in place and for providing useful feedback in a timely manner, all of which have made this book more useful for you, the reader.

Introduction

This book is intended to get beginners and intermediate-level software engineers, up and running with API testing, standard coding practices, and the standards and guidelines for better API test automation development and management.

Each chapter starts by explaining the topic it covers, allowing you to skip ahead if you are already aware of the contents.

Chapter 1 introduces APIs, what API testing is, why we need to have API testing during the software development/testing process, types of API testing, and the advantages of testing APIs.

Chapter 2 explains the different architectures used for developing a scalable software web application plus the protocols used for communicating between the client and the server and their attributes.

Chapter 3 talks about different types of authentication used in web-based software applications.

Chapter 4 covers the tools used in API testing: cURL, Postman, and RestAssured. This chapter also has information on the useful frameworks and libraries used in test automation development.

Chapter 5 introduces the test pyramid and why we need to visualize tests on each layer of a software application.

Chapter 6 walks you through the aspects of API testing and the API testing paradigm.

Chapter 7 talks about the components and guidelines for a good test script.

Chapter 8 covers things that are widely missed and never perceived later in the project life cycle phase, but if used will make test automation much better and joyful.

Chapter 9 talk about the components of the test automation framework and its design aspects. This chapter guides you through writing a test automation framework from scratch.

Chapter 10 is an extension of Chapter 9. In it, you learn how to develop the test script, execute it, and verify the results.

Chapter 11 introduces API documentation developed using the Swagger UI and how to read documentation that will be useful in writing test scripts.

Chapter 12 covers a case study of a shopping cart application of a hypothetical company. A hypothetical character will walk you through the real-life testing working on a Scrum project.

You should have a prior knowledge of the Java programming language and understand the basics of Maven, Tomcat, and Docker. In addition, an awareness of the Spring Framework is good. I use design patterns (Factory pattern, Singleton pattern) and solid design principles in this book so you will gain knowledge on best coding practices.

This book is useful for API testing aspirants and developers/architects. Project managers and non-technical team members will also greatly benefit from reading this book.

The test scripts developed in this book are hosted on GitHub. Any source code or supplementary material referenced by the author in this book is available to readers on GitHub via the book's product page, located at http://www.apress.com/978-1-4842-8141-3. For more detailed information, visit http://www.apress.com/source-code. For any queries or valuable feedback, feel free to get in touch with me, Jagdeep Jain, at jagdeep.jain@gmail.com.

CHAPTER 1

Introduction to API Testing

This chapter introduces application programming interfaces (APIs) and API testing. API testing is an important aspect of software testing activities during the development of typical services-based software. It involves testing the application's business components, usually represented as an API, before the UI is developed. A microservice is an API that deals with a single requirement.

By the end of this chapter, you'll have a good idea of the different types of API testing, the need for them, and the advantages of testing at the API level. If you're already familiar with API testing, you may proceed to the next chapter.

What Is API Testing?

An API abstracts the application layer and provides the resource(s) for consumption by the client. APIs are the backbone of any typical web application, multi-tier web application, or mobile application that hides the inside details of the system, such as how an online payment is processed for a consumer.

APIs are the middle tier of an application and they deal with the back end, usually via an ORM (Object-Relational Mapping) or any other tool, or directly with the database and with the front end. The API acts as an agent

© Jagdeep Jain 2022
J. Jain, *Learn API Testing*, https://doi.org/10.1007/978-1-4842-8142-0_1

between the back end and the front end. The API reads the data from the back end based on the user requirement/request and sends the response to the front end.

For APIs that do not have a front end, the owner of such an API provides a service-based model to their users, such as a payment gateway, weather forecasting, etc.

Figure 1-1 shows a typical service-based software application architecture. It has a database at the back end, APIs in the middle tier, and requests made from a browser or mobile application. We will discuss this setup in detail in the next chapter.

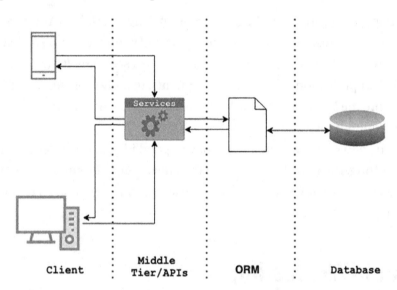

Figure 1-1. *Web-based software application*

A typical web application[1] can be an e-commerce application, where the user wants to see various product offerings and then buy a product as per their needs. Requests are typically made from the front end/GUI. The middle tier has various components in the form of APIs, such as an API

---

[1]https://en.wikipedia.org/wiki/Multitier_architecture

for listing the products based on the requirements of a user, another API to add the product to the e-cart, and another set of APIs or third-party payment APIs to deal with the payment processing on behalf of the e-commerce web store.

A microservice is an API that deals with a single requirement and the service can be functional/deployed independently. Microservices[2] are APIs that define the business logic of a typical software application and fulfill the develop-fast-and-scalable software development philosophy. We will discuss this more in the next chapter.

In the above example of a typical web application, API testing[3] deals with the testing of the APIs for the product listings, adding a product to the e-cart, and performing the payments on behalf of the e-commerce web store.

API testing deals with business workflows. This may be categorized into black-box testing, but technically speaking, it is more of a gray-box testing where the tester knows some internal details of the implementation in brief, but not in depth. They test the APIs individually by having an understanding of the technical aspects of the code path or logic used inside the API.

"Good to have internal knowledge of the implementation for a given API."

API testing is testing the end points[4] of the given API based on the given contract. The endpoint is defined in terms of the URI[5], such as `/api/v1/products/{productId}` or `/api/v1/products`. The contract should be in the required format (`JSON/XML`) of the request, and it may or may not include the parameter(s) based on the request method.

---

[2] `https://en.wikipedia.org/wiki/Microservices`
[3] `https://en.wikipedia.org/wiki/API_testing`
[4] `https://en.wikipedia.org/wiki/Web_API#Endpoints`
[5] `https://en.wikipedia.org/wiki/Uniform_Resource_Identifier`

Accessing an API requires a mechanism that allows us to perform various actions based on the requirement(s), which are called *request methods*[6].

API testing tests the middle tier before it is consumed by the consumer/front end. The tester makes sure that the endpoints are correct and they accept the request in the given format with required parameters and provide the correct response in the prescribed format. This testing directly deals with the application server. It may involve testing the individual component of the application or combining a few components to test a user workflow. All the standard testing techniques are performed while testing APIs, like equivalence class partitions, boundary value analysis, large requests, invalid requests, unauthorized requests, etc.

API testing requires specific tools, such as curl[7], Postman[8], and RestAssured[9], which support the request methods and the protocol that is used to retrieve the API. The commonly used protocol is HTTP(S)[10]. The tester keys in the URL with the required request method and requests the parameters in the API testing tools in the same way as the consumer of the API and then verifies the response/output in the context of the application.

A test plan is required, just like user workflow testing. The test plan has input, expected output, and a precondition.

The concepts in the above paragraphs are covered in more detail in later chapters.

---

[6] https://en.wikipedia.org/wiki/Hypertext_Transfer_Protocol#Request_methods
[7] https://en.wikipedia.org/wiki/CURL
[8] www.postman.com/
[9] https://rest-assured.io/
[10] https://en.wikipedia.org/wiki/Hypertext_Transfer_Protocol

Need

Based on standard software development principles, software should fail fast and quite often before becomes a working product in the development stage. Testing the back end/middle tier is the best way to save time and cost. API testing is the fastest way to find functional/performance/security/(few more types) bugs before a consumer uses it for their own purpose or for GUI development. It is critical for the vendor to test all endpoints since the success or failure of the software application depends on the robustness of the API(s). The business must test all API endpoints efficiently.

The ROI on testing early in the software development process is much higher than testing at the end. Since API testing has larger code/functional coverage, the testing tends to be much more efficient compared to front-end testing. It is faster to identify bugs at the individual API level because the complexity is lower and the possibility of finding bugs is higher compared to finding the bugs on the front-end level.

Not testing the APIs and testing on the front-end level only renders the testing more complex and tedious, and it also usually entails much more testing time and resources. Testing only the front end is an error-prone process. Since the frequency of the changes on the front end tend to be much higher than on the back end/middle tier, the failure rate also tends to be higher. As a result, it's time consuming to identify whether the bug is a back-end/API bug or a front-end bug.

You will see the test pyramid in a later chapter, which will show how efficiently implementing API testing can help reduce testing efforts, save time and cost, and help in building a bug-free product as much as possible (at least without any catastrophic bugs).

Types of API Testing[11]

An API responds to a request by the consumer/front end. The response should be quick. The API should not be allowed to be accessed by an unauthorized user. When concurrent users access the API, it should respond within the stipulated time. Invalid requests to the API should be handled appropriately and an error message should be returned. The API should adhere to the local laws. If the API is provided as a service, then it should maintain the contract with the consumer, the parameter should not change, and so on. All other aspects we discussed are applicable.

The following are the types of API testing:

- Functional testing addresses the functional aspects of the API, such as returning a response as per the business requirements.

- Performance testing addresses the response time under load. When multiple requests are made for the given API at the same point in time, the API should return the response in the allowed time limit as per the SLA definition agreed upon between the service provider and consumer.

- Security testing addresses the unauthorized access of the API by gaining access to the session, parameter tampering, and so on. The API should not allow any anonymous/unauthorized users to gain access to the data via itself.

---

[11] https://en.wikipedia.org/wiki/API_testing#Types_of_API_testing

- Noise testing addresses invalid or malfunction data in the request. The API should respond accordingly and on time. If the data is invalid, the API should respond with the proper error code/message.

- Error code and message testing address incorrect input data and responding with the appropriate error code and message.

- Scale testing is related to infrastructure, which is a DevOps routine job, but the API gets tested in this scenario as well. This is mostly the case in microservices architecture where a particular API is used more frequently. The API should be made scalable since the concurrent access shall be more frequent and the API should be made available all the time.

- Compliance testing falls in the local jurisdiction where the API is being consumed. For example, if the API is asking for personal information (cell number, city of birth, etc.), then this information should be protected by the vendor, any attempt to get this information should not be allowed, and audit logs should be maintained.

- CDCT (consumer-driven contract testing) means that the service provider always maintains the same request payload. This is critical for the business of the service provider. If the payload is changed, then the consumer request will start failing and it will be a loss to the business.

Advantages

Finding bugs at the early stage of software development has advantages. Finding a bug in the back end before the API is implemented saves time in the development of the API. Finding a bug in the middle tier/ API saves time in the development of the front end. The later we test, the more complex and challenging it becomes for the test engineer to find bugs within a tight deadline in the product delivery software development model.

Finding bugs at the business layer facilitates delivery of a quality product. If the API is tested well enough, there are obvious advantages for the product development team.

The following are a few advantages of doing API testing:

1. Easy to automate

2. Faster at finding bugs

3. GUI independent

4. Maximum code path coverage

An API is a simple mechanism. It has an endpoint and a few request methods, The input is the payload, and the output is the response from the API. It is very easy and quick to automate the API tests. Usually, the ratio of GUI vs. API test development is 1:5; that is, you can write five API tests in the same time as one GUI test development. Unlike GUI tests, API tests are not flaky, which means the API contract is not changed and the test never fails. A GUI frequently changes based on end user feedback, but an API does not change unless there is a major change in the business model/ workflow.

It is always faster to find bugs during the development of the business logic. There are a lot of free tools available for testing APIs. It is faster to find bugs even if you are not automating tests from the start of the sprint. Once you have an automation test suite, a developer can run those tests before pushing code to the code repository; also, the issues can be identified on the jenkins build. If the test fails, the developer can always decide on a plan of action to fix the bug or triage the same for the next sprint.

API development is independent of the GUI; the feedback from the tester is faster, and testing can be isolated to the individual API or component level.

An API has greater code path coverage as compared to the GUI. Since the tester tests the business logic at the component level, there is a higher probability of finding bugs and most all code paths are covered. Testing from the GUI is exhaustive if we want to cover all code paths; this leads to different kinds of challenges, like time available for testing and the rate of bug identification.

Summary

In this chapter, you learned what an API is, what API testing is, why you need to test at the API level, various types of API testing, and advantages of doing API testing. In the coming chapters, you will learn that the ROI is beyond your imagination if you test the application at the middle tier—that is, at the API level.

CHAPTER 2

Web Application Architecture

In the previous chapter, you were introduced to API testing. This chapter will help you gain knowledge about the different architectures used for developing a scalable software web application, the protocols used for communicating between a client and a server, and the attributes of those protocols.

At the end of this chapter, you should have a good idea of monolithic and microservices-based architecture and RESTful architecture, the communication established between client and server, and HTTP, headers, requests, and responses. If you are already familiar with web-based software application architecture, you can proceed to the next chapter.

Web Applications Defined

A web application is software that runs on a browser. A web application addresses specific needs for the user, such as booking airline tickets. Each web application is developed based with a business goal, user base, and future in mind. Accordingly, its architecture is decided. For a tester, it is very important to have an understanding of the underlying architecture and its various aspects, like protocol stack, communication medium between client and server, and attributes.

© Jagdeep Jain 2022
J. Jain, *Learn API Testing*, https://doi.org/10.1007/978-1-4842-8142-0_2

With the evolution of the Web, various architectures came into existence. In the context of API testing, we will be discussing a few important types that exist as of now.

Monolithic vs. Microservices Architecture

Instead of discussing monolithic and microservices architecture types separately, we will discuss the differences, which will help in your quick understanding.

Software applications have evolved over a few decades. Everyone who develops and maintains software ends up finding new ways of doing things or organizing stuff in a way to tackle future problems.

Software development teams are always under pressure to deliver quickly in order to beat the competition. This leads to messed-up code quite often. (More accurately, it is always the case.) A monolithic application is an example of fast development, where the development team wants to develop the product in a quick turnaround time. They write everything in a single bundle and deliver it to the customer. It works well for a couple of months or a year or two, and then requirements are floated from the customer that require a change in the design or architecture.

Agile development supports changing the design/architecture over a period of time while delivering the code and deploying it to production with each iteration.

To deal with complexity and at the same time support the idea of delivering faster, a new architecture was proposed by the brilliant engineers in our software industry. It led to defining specific properties for each business component and having a dedicated service. An individual business component or a single responsibility service is called a microservice. In a big software application, multiple services work together to accomplish a single goal that enables business.

Each microservice is independent of each other and has no impact on the other microservices in any manner whatsoever.

Monolithic architecture is shown in Figure 2-1.

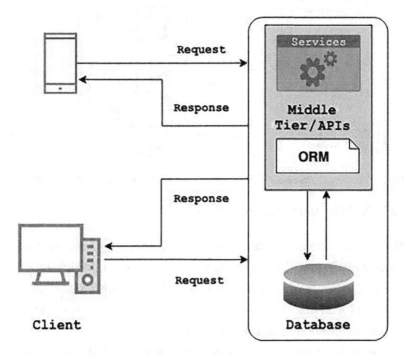

Figure 2-1. *Monolithic architecture*

Monolithic applications have a single instance. They are tightly coupled and have a single datasource (usually). They have a single deployable code base.

Microservices architecture is shown in Figure 2-2.

13

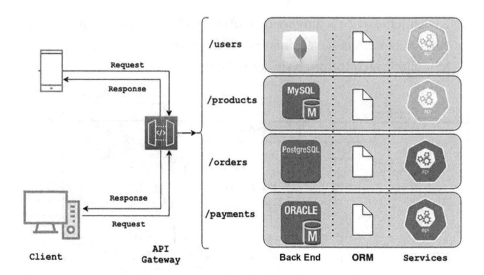

Figure 2-2. *Microservices architecture*

Microservices architecture consists of multiple deployments. Each deployment is uniquely identified by a service name/endpoint. All of the services are loosely coupled and have their own datasource (strictly). Each service is deployed in a way that other services are not aware of, or the deployment is independent of each other.

Hibernate[1] is a typical example of Object Relational Mapping that ties the database to the services in a programmer-friendly manner.

There is also a micro front end where we have the liberty to deploy and manage the module-specific front end (a micro front end discussion is out of scope of this book). Table 2-1 compares monolithic vs. microservices-based architectures.

---

[1] https://en.wikipedia.org/wiki/Hibernate_(framework)

Table 2-1. *Differences Between Monolithic vs. Microservices Architecture*

Categories	Monolithic	Microservices	Notes
Initial setup	✓	✓	Microservices come with infrastructure requirements so initial setup takes time.
Faster development		✓	Since the microservices are independent, each team can work independently without worrying about any factors related to other microservices whereas monolithic application code is complex since everyone is working on the same code base.
Maintenance		✓	A microservices application has low maintenance but infrastructure maintenance is required.
Deployment		✓	A monolithic application has a single deployment, though it may be tedious, but compared to microservices, the difference is in infrastructural changes.

(*continued*)

Table 2-1. (*continued*)

Categories	Monolithic	Microservices	Notes
Enhancements		☑	Adding a new feature to a monolithic application requires a lot of thought since existing designs may not support new features and changes often come with a risk factor. Microservices are independent, so any new enhancement/addition of a service tends to be straightforward.
Performance	☑		A monolithic application has the advantage here since multiple instances can be run simultaneously compared to microservices. However, it comes with other challenges.
Security	☑		Security is a one-time setup for a monolithic application.
Ease of use		☑	A microservices application has an advantage here. If, for example, there are performance issues in one service, this will not impact the entire application. The user can still use the other workflows. But with monolithic applications, the entire application is at risk since it is a single deployment.

(*continued*)

Table 2-1. (*continued*)

Categories	Monolithic	Microservices	Notes
Adaptability to latest tech stack		☑	Microservices can adapt to the latest tech stack since they are independent. So, the team can decide and choose the best-suited tools for their needs.
Debugging and testing	☑		Since all code is at one place in a monolithic application, it is easier to debug and test.
End-to-end testing	☑		End-to-end testing is easier in monolithic applications compared to microservices-based applications, where end-to-end testing is necessary on the user interface.

Now that you understand that the architecture of a typical web application that runs over web services/APIs, you can design test strategies accordingly.

Designing Test Strategies

Testing a monolithic web application is easier than testing a microservice. To test a microservice, you need to implement additional stubs and/or mock the APIs for end-to-end testing.

In the rest of the book, you will be using a monolithic web application to learn API testing. You will review RESTful, HTTP, headers, requests, and responses in the remaining sections to ensure you have a solid foundation when working with monolithic web apps in future chapters.

A typical REST application architecture is shown in Figure 2-3.

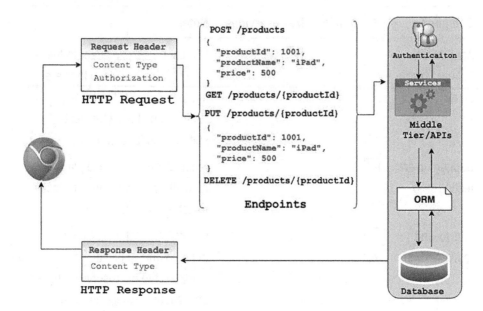

Figure 2-3. *REST application architecture*

RESTful Architecture

REST stands for REpresentational State Transfer. A REST service meets the RESTful constraints called a RESTful service. Roy Fielding[2] introduced RESTful architecture in 2000.

The Web has evolved over a period of time from Web 1.0 to 2.0, 3.0, and towards 4.0[3]. Web 1.0 is for document sharing. Web 2.0 is people-centric and supports the Internet as a platform. Web 3.0 is an executable web that supports data sharing. Web 4.0 is a smart and intelligent web where machines are smart enough to load content for humans.

---

[2] https://en.wikipedia.org/wiki/Roy_Fielding
[3] https://ijcsit.com/docs/Volume%205/vol5issue06/ijcsit20140506265.pdf

When developing a web application for the World Wide Web, the architecture should meet the growing needs and must include the following non-functional requirements:

- Efficiency

- Performance and scalability

- Reliability

- Reusability

- Portability

- Modularity

...and a few more.

RESTful architecture is for software engineers. It addresses the non-functional requirements by putting some constraints on developing an API.

A REST service that meet the constraints of RESTful[4] architecture is called a RESTful service. The constraints are as follows:

- Client-server architecture

- Statelessness

- Cacheability

- Use of a layered system

- Uniform interface

- Support for code on demand

Client-server architecture supports the separation of responsibilities. The client is independent of the server. The client or the user interface can be developed independently without knowing the internal details of the server and its functions.

---

[4] https://en.wikipedia.org/wiki/Representational_state_transfer

Statelessness helps in improving the overall performance of the server. The server is not required to know or maintain the state/session of the request. Its basic job is to provide the response without tracking the source with a session. This is achieved by the HTTP protocol.

Caching helps in improving the performance. If the same request is coming from various users, it can be cached. HTTP has a feature that helps in caching the responses. This helps the server to be more efficient.

Using a layered system helps in addressing a few more concerns like authentication and security. Having a layered system is beneficial for debugging the root cause quickly.

A uniform interface is fundamental to the RESTful architecture. It ensures that resources are identified based on the URI, such as /api/v1/products. With respect to the uniform interface, it is good to go through HATEOAS[5] once.

Examples of support for code-on-demand are Java applets or client-side JavaScripts. Having the above understanding is enough for testing RESTful APIs. RESTful architecture uses HTTP as the protocol for communication between the client and the server. Since HTTP is a stateless protocol, RESTful architecture aims for scalability and performance, and since HTTP internally calls TCP for the connection between client and server, it is reliable as well. Let's discuss HTTP in detail in the next section.

HTTP

Hypertext Transfer Protocol (HTTP) is used for communication between the client and the server in a typical web application.

HTTP exhibits RESTful architectural requirements.

---

[5] https://en.wikipedia.org/wiki/HATEOAS

The first basic version was HTTP 0.9. Later, with few updates, it was released as HTTP 1.0. This version utilizes a separate connection for each request.

The HTTP 1.1 version is the most popular and widely used version as of now. This version solves the latency issue. The header metadata and the message are in text format. HTTP 2.0 offers performance optimization on the header metadata by using encryption; also, the message is multiplexed between the client and the server for better performance. HTTP 3.0 is currently under development; it uses UDP as the transport layer.

You will be using HTTP 1.1 throughout this book.

HTTP is an application layer[6] protocol that works over a TCP (http:// default port 80) or TLS[7] (https:// over port 443) encrypted TCP connection. TCP is the most reliable protocol; it is guaranteed that the packets will be sent/received 100% without any loss. In case of loss, an error message will be sent to the receiver.

The HTTP protocol fetches the resource from the server based on the request, such as fetching the HTML contents from the server or data in a specified format. Before HTTP fetches the data from the server, the client has to establish a connection with the server in order to fetch the resources over HTTP. This is done by three-way communication between the client and the server over a TCP layer. The client sends a connection request on a given port to the server. The server acknowledges that the request is received and then the client acknowledges the same. This way a connection is established between the client and the server. Now with HTTP, the client can fetch the required information from the server. Once the connection is established, the client can send multiple requests over HTTP and the server will send the response to each request.

---

[6]https://en.wikipedia.org/wiki/Application_layer
[7]https://en.wikipedia.org/wiki/Transport_Layer_Security

The HTTP protocol is simple, extensible, and stateless. We can read the headers and the message body. In case of a change in the header(s) usage or semantics, it can be adapted easily between the client and the server. The server does not remember the state of the request. It just sends the requested data and opens for new requests.

HTTP supports a caching mechanism. Clients can send information in the request header to store the response in a cache for a stipulated amount of time for later use for faster performance. HTTP also supports CORS[8]; that is, if the request body or the HTML has a different domain, this will be served to the client. HTTP also works on `sessionId`. The client sends a request and the server sends the `sessionId` in response. Later, this `sessionId` can be used to authenticate the request. A typical server has a proxy in between to hide the server IP from hackers. HTTP supports proxy servers that mimic the real server in real time.

Figure 2-4 summarizes the steps of an HTTP connection between the client and the web server. Step 1 establishes the TCP connection between the client and the server. Step 2 fetches the resources from the server over HTTP. With a single TCP connection, a client can send multiple requests and the server will respond to the required information over HTTP.

---

[8] https://en.wikipedia.org/wiki/Cross-origin_resource_sharing

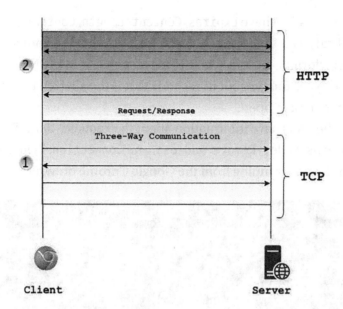

Figure 2-4. *Client-server communication*

Headers

Headers are a part of each HTTP request/response, and they define the flow of the information between the client and server. The most common fields in headers[9] are Content Type, Content Length, Host, User-Agent, Accept, Accept Encoding, Accept Language, Connection, Cache Control, Age, Date, Expires, and Keep-Alive.

Headers are logically grouped into three categories: request headers, response headers, and general headers. This can be seen in the network tab of the browser after sending the request.

Request headers mainly have Authorization, Host, Accept, Accept-Language, Accept-Encoding, and Content-Type fields. The Authorization field is used for authentication with the server. It specifies that the request is coming from the authorized client.

---

[9]https://en.wikipedia.org/wiki/List_of_HTTP_header_fields

23

Response headers have Expires, Content-Length, Content-Type, Cache-Control, Date, and Keep-Alive fields. Content-Type provides the response type format, such as whether the response is in JSON or plain text. Keep-Alive is the timeout in seconds that is the allowed time for a connection to remain open.

General headers have information about the Request URL, Request Method, Status Code, Remote Address, and Connection. Figure 2-5 depicts the Header grouping from the Google Chrome browser.

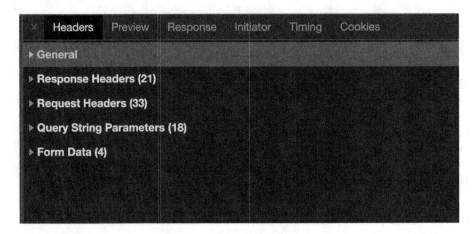

Figure 2-5. *HTTP headers in the Google Chrome Network tab*

There is one more category of headers named representation headers, with Content-Type, Content-Length, and other fields related to the presentation of the response.

Most of the fields are self-explanatory and do not require detailed discussion. From the API testing point of view, it is critical to know the most commonly used header fields, which are mentioned in this section. You will see headers in action in the coming chapters.

Requests

The client starts communication with the server using an HTTP request. The request has a request method, resource address (on the server) URI, request header(s), and a request body, which is optional.

Request Methods

Request methods are the actions that the client wants to perform on the server resource. The most common methods used in developing API-based software applications are GET, POST, PUT, and DELETE. Others are TRACE, UPDATE, HEAD, CONNECT, OPTIONS, TRACE, and PATCH.

The GET method is used to retrieve the information from the server. The POST method is used to add a new object to the server resource. The PUT method is used to update the existing object on the server resource. The DELETE method is used to delete the object on the server resource. GET, PUT, and DELETE are idempotent methods; that is, if you execute the same call multiple times, the result will be the same. GET is also a safe method where no harm is made if you execute the call multiple times.

Resource Addresses

A resource address is defined by a URI, where URI stands for Uniform Resource Identifier. It is the identifier of the resource on the server, called as the endpoint of the service, such as /api/v1/products.

Request Headers

A request header contains an authentication field, which authenticates the request on the server, and Content-Type, which specifies the type of content expected from the server resource. (There are other headers based on the requirements.) You will learn about standard authentications in the next chapter.

Request Body

The request body has a format to be followed, which is understood by the server resource or the service endpoint. Usually, the response body is in a JSON or XML format.

Table 2-2 shows an example of a GET request. In this request, the endpoint returns the list of the products, so the request body is not required.

Table 2-2. *HTTP GET Request*

Request line	**GET, /api/v1/products**
Request headers	**Authentication : Bearer** eyJhbGciO...
Request body	

Table 2-3 shows an example of a POST request. The request message will look like below. Since you are creating an object on the server resource, the request body has the details about the object that needs to be created.

Table 2-3. *HTTP POST Request*

Request line	**POST, /api/v1/products**
Request headers	**Authentication : Bearer** eyJhbGciO...

Request body	```{
	    "productId": 1001,
	    "product_name": "iPad",
	    "product_price": 500
	}```

Table 2-4 offers an example of a PUT request that is updating the product price for productId 1001.

Table 2-4. *HTTP PUT Request*

Request line	PUT, **/api/v1/products/1001**
Request headers	**Authentication : Bearer** eyJhbGciO...

Request body	**{**
	    "productId": 1001,
	    "product_price": 700
	}

Table 2-5 shows an example of a DELETE request. Here you are deleting productId 1001. You don't need the request body, so it is empty.

Table 2-5. *HTTP DELETE Request*

Request line	DELETE, **/api/v1/products/1001**
Request headers	**Authentication : Bearer** eyJhbGciO...
Request body	

Response

When the request reaches the server, it sends the response. The protocol used here is HTTP. It has a status line, response headers, and a message body.

Status Line

The status line lists the protocol version, the return status code, and the status text. We will discuss status codes in the next section. Status codes are commonly known as response codes.

Response Header

The response header contains the information sent by the server to define the response message, such as Content-Length and Content-Type.

Response Body

The response body is the response message that is sent by the server to the client based on the request on the given resource. Table 2-6 presents an example of a GET request. The server found the resource and it has returned the response with success.

Table 2-6. *HTTP GET Response*

Status line	**HTTP/1.1 200 OK**
Response header	**Content-Type : application/json**
Response body	**{**
	** "productId": 1001,**
	** "product_name": "iPad",**
	** "product_price": 500**
	}

For all request methods, the HTTP response has the same format of status line, response headers, and a response body.

Response Codes

HTTP responses have a status line that contains the status code of the response. From the response code we can understand if the response from the server is successful or not. Response codes are grouped in various classes based on the characteristics of the response. The most common groupings are as follows:

- Information: 1XX-199

- Success: 2XX-299

- Redirect: 3XX-399

- Error from client: 4XX-499

- Error from server: 5XX-599

A few examples of status codes are as follows:

- The 102 status code in the status line signifies that the request from the client is received and the server is working on the response.

- The 200 status code signifies that the request from the client is successful and accepted by the server.

- The 302 status code signifies that the request is redirected to another resource.

- The 400 status code signifies that the request from the client is erroneous.

- The 500 status code signifies that the server is not reachable or there is a server error.

The list is big[10], but you just need to remember the few that are commonly used in API-based software applications. Knowing the response code is important for API testing because the consumer of the API should know the response from the server, and in case of error, corrective actions can be made.

---

[10] https://en.wikipedia.org/wiki/List_of_HTTP_status_codes

Summary

In this chapter, you learned about web-based application architecture types, which are commonly used industry wide. You also went through the communication aspects between a client and server and those attributes. You learned about HTTP, HTTP headers, HTTP requests, HTTP responses, and various response codes in a typical web-based application. In the next chapter, you will learn about standard authentications.

CHAPTER 3

Authentication

This chapter will help you gain knowledge about the different types of authentications used in web-based software applications.

By the end of this chapter, you should have a good idea of the standard authentication mechanism used in developing web-based applications. You will also get an idea about authorization mechanisms. If you are already familiar with these concepts, you may proceed to the next chapter.

Authentication is a way to verify a user before they log into an application, and authorization defines what the user can access. Consider a person who buys an economy class plane ticket to Honolulu, Hawaii. They go to the airport and the ground staff checks their ticket and passport for (identity) authentication to verify their entitlement to board a particular flight. When they enter the plane, the staff directs them to economy class seating because they are not authorized to sit in the business class seats.

For API testing, you will be targeting HTTP authentication and a little bit of authorization.

HTTP Authentication

Let's go over the most commonly used HTTP authentication types for accessing an API.

Basic Authentication

HTTP basic authentication[1] is a very simple authentication mechanism to access APIs. The user agent sends the username and password encoded in a variant of Base64[2] (RFC7617). This is not encrypted but merely encoded.

The username and password can be passed in a header request as follows:

```
Authorization: Basic amFnZGVlcDpoZXN0MTIz
```

You can also pass the username and password as a parameter from a user agent like Postman. This is not secure and can be easily hacked by anyone who has a little knowledge of gathering keystrokes.

Session-Based Authentication

For accessing resources on the server over HTTP, the client reserves a session with an identification on the server and further communication is established using the same identification. The server sends a SESSIONID in the header response to the client and further communication is established based on the SESSIONID on the server.

In a Java-based application, the server sends a cookie in the header response as shown:

```
Set-Cookie: JSESSIONID=B6A7F58E7F5AC8FE2B1C6F8E15F93E84;
```

The client uses this session identification and sends it in a header request as a cookie to access the API resources.

```
Cookie: JSESSIONID=B6A7F58E7F5AC8FE2B1C6F8E15F93E84
```

---

[1] From: Sai Matam and Jagdeep Jain, *Pro Apache JMeter* (Apress, 2017)
[2] www.base64encode.org/

Sessions are short lived, and we can set the expiration time in the header. This method is mostly used in shopping cart applications where a session is established between the client and the server until the user performs the payment, closes the browser, or the session is invalidated.

Another method is URL rewriting. This is an insecure way of communicating with the server. If a hacker gets hold of the `SESSIONID`, they can do things as per their free will.

Token/JWT-Based Authentication

A user logs into the application using the credentials and gets a token to access the application. The token is valid for a certain period of time, so accessing it after the time limit requires a new token to be generated by the server. It is like a ticket to a movie theater where you have access to a certain movie for a certain period of time.

A token supports a stateless connection over HTTP where the server sends the token to the client as a header response. After that, each time the client requests a resource, the token needs to be sent in the header.

The server sends the token in the response header on the `/auth` (authenticating a user) call.

```
Authorization: eyJhbGciOiJIUzI1NiJ9.eyJzdWIiOiJhZG1pbiIsImV4c
CI6MTYzODgxNDQxNSwiaWF0IjoxNjM4ODEyNjE1fQ.UVAmFYlDnoX5GhF987
Wz8pObABDoHWI7KujPCb99x-8
```

The client sends the bearer token in the request header, as shown:

```
Authorization: Bearer eyJhbGciOiJIUzI1NiJ9.eyJzdWIiOiJhZG1pbi
IsImV4cCI6MTYzODgxNDQxNSwiaWF0IjoxNjM4ODEyNjE1fQ.UVAmFYlDnoX
5GhF987Wz8pObABDoHWI7KujPCb99x-8
```

This says that the bearer of the token should be given access to the server resources. The server does not need to remember the session or the state. Instead, this is taken care of by the client via the token. This helps in improving the performance of the server.

JWT stands for JSON Web Token. It is one of the formats of the token formed by the server. It is defined as an open standard in RFC7519 as transmitting information between the client and the server via a JSON object. JSON is lightweight and less verbose compared to the other formats and is a preferred token-based authentication format.

Look at the two dots in the JWT. It has three parts: header, payload, and signature. Figure 3-1 presents a screenshot of jwt.io[3] and shows the decoded token.

Figure 3-1. *JWT Decoder jwt.io*

---

[3] https://jwt.io/

The jwt.io screenshot is self-explanatory. The header contains the algorithm and the token type. The payload is the data. The signature makes sure that the data has not changed during transit.

OAuth2-Based Authentication

Basic and session-based authentications are not reliable and are not the most robust ways of undertaking authentication. They may lead to various problems in terms of security and performance.

The OAuth framework was developed for ease of use, better security, and better access control of the resources on the server.

OAuth 1.0 is the first version of the OAuth protocol. OAuth 2.0[4] (RFC6749) was developed after the identification of the limitations and drawbacks of earlier versions. OAuth 2.0 is completely different from OAuth 1.0. It is a full rewrite and is not backward compatible.

OAuth 2.0 introduces a layer for authorization in the workflow of a typical usage of the service, or the API endpoint, or the server resource. It also introduces terminology called *roles* to make it easier for developers.

These roles are as follows:

- **Client**: A user-agent, such as a browser or a mobile device, from which the request is made to access the resources on the server

- **Resource owner**: The actual user who owns the resources on the server, or who has access permission on the server

---

[4] https://datatracker.ietf.org/doc/html/rfc6749

- **Authorization server**: The layer that separates the client and the resource owner. This server provides the access token to the client or the user-agent through which the client or the user-agent gains access to the resources on the server.

- **Resource server or resource provider**: The server where resources are kept, or the API endpoints through which resources can be accessed

In Figure 3-2, the user-agent requests authorization from the resource owner, and the resource owner provides the grant to the user agent.

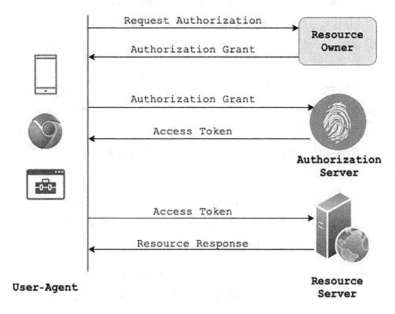

Figure 3-2. *Token-based authorization*

The user-agent then goes to the authorization server to get the access token, and the authorization server provides the access token. The user-agent requests the resource from the server with the access token, and the resource server provides the required response to the user-agent.

OAuth 2.0 has an additional workflow known as a refresh token. When the token expires, the user-agent uses the refresh token to get the new access token.

OAuth 2.0 uses JWT as a token format and uses an authorization header with a bearer token just like JWT.

With OAuth, we conclude discussion on authentication types.

You have gone through old and new authentication types used in web application development. Having a good knowledge of the authentication types makes the job of testing the endpoints much easier. In the next section, we will briefly discuss the standard authorization used in the industry.

Authorization

Authorization helps organizations manage resources among various user types as per their respective work profiles. This is helpful in various ways for a user, an employee, and an organization. We will discuss the most widely used authorization types in the sections below.

RBAC

RBAC stands for role-based access control. In a typical software application, access to the users is granted based on their role in the organization. For a CRM application, the sales and marketing team has a different role than the stores, operations, or finance teams. Admin may not have visibility to these departments but can manage the roles and permissions. A few may have view-only permission while others may have write permission as well.

RBAC is very commonly used industry wide. It is suitable for organizations of all sizes, be they very small or very large. It offers several advantages, such as accessing, security risk assessment and management, in addition to significant improvements in employee productivity, communication, and collaboration.

RBAC helps in assigning users certain roles and assigning permission levels to each role. A user can have different roles and a role can have different permissions.

With respect to API testing, we can make sure that the user who does have write permission can do CRUD operations, and the user who doesn't have write permission cannot.

ABAC

ABAC stands for attribute-based access control. It is an alternative to RBAC. In this authorization type, the user is granted a role based on an attribute. For example, only employees in the Asia Pacific region can access APAC region files. Others are denied access upon trying to access the files of the APAC region.

Authentication and authorization are vast topics, and a dedicated book can be written on them. We will limit our discussion based on our requirements.

Authentication and Authorization Services

Authentication and authorization services are provided by a few vendors. Okta, RSA, and Ping Identity are few who provide IAM (Identity Access Management) as a service. These services are used by various software companies and thus save development cost and resources time.

Google, Twitter, and Microsoft use OAuth 2.0 for authentication of their services. These companies also provide authentication for third-party user-agents/applications.

Summary

In this chapter, you learned about standard authentication and authorization used in developing web-based applications. You now know about the various authentication types used by APIs for user authentication as well as a little bit on authorization. In the next chapter, you will use your knowledge from the first three chapters and perform testing on the APIs for a contact management application.

CHAPTER 4

Tools, Frameworks, and Libraries

This chapter will help you gain insight into the tools used for testing API-based software applications and writing test automation scripts. In this chapter, you will also explore the useful frameworks and libraries used in test automation script development.

Before starting this chapter, you should read Appendix B and deploy the sample application that you will be using as a demo application for testing. Also, you should go through the API endpoints provided in the sample application that you will be using to learn API testing with industry-standard tools.

At the end of this chapter, you should have a good idea of the standard API testing applications, frameworks, and libraries that are used to test and write automation test scripts.

To write software applications, we use an IDE (integrated development environment). It is a daily job for a software developer to write new code in an IDE and debug the issues reported by the testing engineer. There are API testing applications that have made the testing of APIs very easy. You just need to add a few things to configure a test in the tool and you can test API endpoints. In this book, you will use Java as the test automation language to write a standard test automation script. You can, however, use any other language at your discretion.

© Jagdeep Jain 2022
J. Jain, *Learn API Testing*, https://doi.org/10.1007/978-1-4842-8142-0_4

For quick API testing, you could use one of the standard software applications we will be discussing in the sections below. Also, for writing a standard test script, you will go through a few frameworks and libraries, which you will be using in the upcoming chapters to write a testing framework.

API Testing Tools

Let's explore the software/tools used industry-wide for testing API endpoints. cURL is a Linux tool. Postman is a browser/desktop-based software application. RestAssured is an open source Java-based framework for writing BDT (behavior-driven testing) scripts.

Let's discuss each of these in the sections below.

cURL

Client URL (cURL) is a Linux tool for communication between two machines. It is the most common command line tool for testing APIs. Let's discuss how to use this tool for API endpoint testing. Mostly it is used by developers to quickly test the API they are developing.

Every application requires authentication before accessing its resource(s). You will start with authentication and then use common HTTP methods with cURL to verify the response. This tool can be mixed with various programming languages as well for automation testing.

Authentication

For RESTful services, which have an authentication server that authenticates the user, a token is generated to access the resource on the server. This must be passed as a bearer token for authentication using a cURL command.

For contact management services, the authentication endpoint is /
auth/authenticate.

Since it is a POST method, you need to pass the required arguments to
the cURL command.

Once the application is ready, enter the following command in the
terminal window to get the bearer token:

```
$ curl -d '{"userName": "admin", "password": "test123"}'
-H 'Content-Type: application/json' http://localhost:8080/app/
auth/authenticate -v
```

-d is used to pass the data.

-H is used to pass metadata in the header.

-v is used for verbose and it contains the header response and the
authorization bearer token.

The following is the response, including the headers. The authorization
token is highlighted in bold.

```
*   Trying ::1...
* TCP_NODELAY set
* Connected to localhost (::1) port 8080 (#0)
> POST /app/auth/authenticate HTTP/1.1
> Host: localhost:8080
> User-Agent: curl/7.64.1
> Accept: */*
> Content-Type: application/json
> Content-Length: 44
>
* upload completely sent off: 44 out of 44 bytes
< HTTP/1.1 200
< Authorization: eyJhbGciOiJIUzI1NiJ9.eyJzdWIiOiJhZG1pbiIs
  ImV4cCI6MTY0ODk2OTk0MiwiaWF0IjoxNjQ0OTY4MTEyfQ.VDbBzHLjjfDJg
  MmYZHwbR_l36l__OZKy5XK8vhT3cZM
```

```
< Content-Type: application/json;charset=UTF-8
< Transfer-Encoding: chunked
< Date: Sun, 03 Apr 2022 06:41:52 GMT
<
* Connection #0 to host localhost left intact
{"password":"$2a$10$cyztG895P5ViBcTF7WM60eQ7TRreIvXdNc/WWIgBIQT
563PhOyCGe","username":"admin","enabled":true,"authorities":
[{"authority":"ROLE_ADMIN"},{"authority":"ROLE_USER"},
{"authority":"ROLE_MGR"}],"accountNonExpired":true,"account
NonLocked":true,"credentialsNonExpired":true}* Closing
connection 0
```

POST

The POST method has a payload that is sent to the server from the client.
You also need to pass the token while sending the request. Copy the token
from the output of the above command and pass in the POST command.

Once the application is started, enter the following command in the
terminal window:

```
$ curl -d '{ "firstName": "Firstname", "lastName":
"Lastname", "email": "firstname@fl-testing.com"}' -H
'Content-Type: application/json' -H 'Authorization: Bearer
eyJhbGciOiJIUzI1NiJ9.eyJzdWIiOiJhZG1pbiIsImV4cCI6MTY0ODk
2OTkxMiwiaWF0IjoxNjQ4OTY4MTEyfQ.VDbBzHLjjfDJgMmYZHwbR_
l36l__0ZKy5XK8vhT3cZM' http://localhost:8080/app/api/v1/
contacts -v
```

-d is used to pass the data; this is the payload for adding the contact to
the contact management application.

-H is used to pass metadata in the header; you are passing a bearer
token in the header for authentication.

-v is used for verbose.

The following is the response, including the headers:

```
*   Trying ::1...
* TCP_NODELAY set
* Connected to localhost (::1) port 8080 (#0)
> POST /app/api/v1/contacts HTTP/1.1
> Host: localhost:8080
> User-Agent: curl/7.64.1
> Accept: */*
> Content-Type: application/json
> Authorization: Bearer eyJhbGciOiJIUzI1NiJ9.eyJzdWIiOiJhZG1
  pbiIsImV4cCI6MTY0ODk2OTkxMiwiaWF0IjoxNjQ0OTY4MTEyfQ.VDbBzHLjj
  fDJgMmYZHwbR_l36l__OZKy5XK8vhT3cZM
> Content-Length: 88
>
* upload completely sent off: 88 out of 88 bytes
< HTTP/1.1 201
< Location: http://localhost:8080/app/api/v1/contacts/1004
< X-Content-Type-Options: nosniff
< X-XSS-Protection: 1; mode=block
< Cache-Control: no-cache, no-store, max-age=0, must-revalidate
< Pragma: no-cache
< Expires: 0
< X-Frame-Options: DENY
< Transfer-Encoding: chunked
< Date: Sun, 03 Apr 2022 06:51:43 GMT
<
* Connection #0 to host localhost left intact
* Closing connection 0
```

The 20X response signifies that the POST request is successful, and the record is created as per the payload.

In the following section, you'll verify using a GET call if the record is added successfully or not.

GET

The GET method is usually used for retrieving information from the server. You also need to pass the token while sending the request. The API expects the contactId; you will pass the contactId of the contact created with the help of the POST request.

Once the application is started, enter the following command in the terminal window:

```
$ curl -H 'Content-Type: application/json' -H 'Authorization:
Bearer eyJhbGciOiJIUzI1NiJ9.eyJzdWIiOiJhZG1pbiIsImV4cCI6M
TY0ODk2OTkxMiwiaWF0IjoxNjQ4OTY4MTEyfQ.VDbBzHLjjfDJgMmYZHwbR_
l36l__oZKy5XK8vhT3cZM' http://localhost:8080/app/api/v1/
contacts/1004 -v
```

-H is used to pass metadata in the header; you are passing a bearer token in the header for authentication.

-v is used for verbose.

The following is the response, including the headers:

```
*   Trying ::1...
* TCP_NODELAY set
* Connected to localhost (::1) port 8080 (#0)
> GET /app/api/v1/contacts/1004 HTTP/1.1
> Host: localhost:8080
> User-Agent: curl/7.64.1
> Accept: */*
> Content-Type: application/json
```

```
> Authorization: Bearer eyJhbGciOiJIUzI1NiJ9.eyJzdWIiOiJhZG
  1pbiIsImV4cCI6MTYwODk2OTkxMiwiaWF0IjoxNjQ0OTY4MTEyfQ.VDbBzHLjj
  fDJgMmYZHwbR_l36l__oZKy5XK8vhT3cZM
>
< HTTP/1.1 200
< X-Content-Type-Options: nosniff
< X-XSS-Protection: 1; mode=block
< Cache-Control: no-cache, no-store, max-age=0, must-revalidate
< Pragma: no-cache
< Expires: 0
< X-Frame-Options: DENY
< Content-Type: application/json;charset=UTF-8
< Transfer-Encoding: chunked
< Date: Sun, 03 Apr 2022 06:58:36 GMT
<
* Connection #0 to host localhost left intact
{"id":1004,"firstName":"Firstname","lastName":"Lastname",
"email":"firstname@fl-testing.com"}* Closing connection 0
```

The 200 response signifies the success of the GET request with the contact being retrieved, which you created using the POST method.

In the following section, you'll update this record using the PUT method.

PUT

The PUT method is usually used for updating the record on the server. You also need to pass the token while sending the request.

The record you created has an id of 1004. Therefore, you need to pass the id on the URL to inform the server that this id needs to be updated.

Once the application is started, enter the following command in the terminal window:

```
$ curl -d '{ "firstName": "Sudeep", "lastName": "Tripathy",
"email": "st@learn-api-testing.com"}' -H 'Content-Type:
application/json' -H 'Authorization: Bearer eyJhbGciOiJIUzI1
NiJ9.eyJzdWIiOiJhZG1pbiIsImV4cCI6MTY0ODk2OTkxMiwiaWF0IjoxNjQ40
TY4MTEyfQ.VDbBzHLjjfDJgMmYZHwbR_l36l__oZKy5XK8vhT3cZM' -X PUT
http://localhost:8080/app/api/v1/contacts/1004 -v
```

-d is used to pass the data; it is the payload for adding the contact to the contact management application.

-H is used to pass metadata in the header; you are passing the bearer token in the header for authentication.

-X is used to notify the cURL command that is called with the specific method to be executed on the server; you also add PUT in the call to make sure the server understands it as an update operation.

-v is used for verbose.

The following is the response, including the headers:

```
*   Trying ::1...
* TCP_NODELAY set
* Connected to localhost (::1) port 8080 (#0)
> PUT /app/api/v1/contacts/1004 HTTP/1.1
> Host: localhost:8080
> User-Agent: curl/7.64.1
> Accept: */*
> Content-Type: application/json
> Authorization: Bearer eyJhbGciOiJIUzI1NiJ9.eyJzdWIiOiJhZG1p
  biIsImV4cCI6MTY0ODk2OTkxMiwiaWF0IjoxNjQ40TY4MTEyfQ.VDbBzH
  LjjfDJgMmYZHwbR_l36l__oZKy5XK8vhT3cZM
> Content-Length: 85
>
```

```
* upload completely sent off: 85 out of 85 bytes
< HTTP/1.1 200
< Location: http://localhost:8080/app/api/v1/contacts/1004
< X-Content-Type-Options: nosniff
< X-XSS-Protection: 1; mode=block
< Cache-Control: no-cache, no-store, max-age=0, must-revalidate
< Pragma: no-cache
< Expires: 0
< X-Frame-Options: DENY
< Transfer-Encoding: chunked
< Date: Sun, 03 Apr 2022 07:05:44 GMT
<
* Connection #0 to host localhost left intact
* Closing connection 0
```

The 200 response signifies that the PUT request is successful so you have successfully updated the resource on the server. This can be verified by using the GET call.

In the next section, you'll delete this record using the DELETE method.

DELETE

The DELETE method is usually used for deleting the record on the server. You also need to pass the token while sending the request.

The record you created has the id of 1000, so you need to pass the id on the URL to inform the server that the record with this id needs to be deleted.

Once the application starts, enter the following command in the terminal window:

```
$ curl -H 'Authorization: Bearer eyJhbGciOiJIUzI1NiJ9.eyJzdWIiO
iJhZG1pbiIsImV4cCI6MTY0ODk2OTkxMiwiaWF0IjoxNjQ4OTY4MTEyfQ.
VDbBzHLjjfDJgMmYZHwbR_l36l__0ZKy5XK8vhT3cZM' -X DELETE http://
localhost:8080/app/api/v1/contacts/1004 -v
```

-H is used to pass metadata in the header; you are passing bearer token in the header for authentication.

-X is used to notify the cURL command that is called with the specific method to be executed on the server; you also add DELETE in the call to make sure the server understands it as a delete operation.

-v is used for verbose.

The following is the response, including the headers:

```
*   Trying ::1...
* TCP_NODELAY set
* Connected to localhost (::1) port 8080 (#0)
> DELETE /app/api/v1/contacts/1004 HTTP/1.1
> Host: localhost:8080
> User-Agent: curl/7.64.1
> Accept: */*
> Authorization: Bearer eyJhbGciOiJIUzI1NiJ9.eyJzdWIiOiJh
  ZG1pbiIsImV4cCI6MTY0ODk2OTkxMiwiaWF0IjoxNjQ4OTY4MTEyfQ.
  VDbBzHLjjfDJgMmYZHwbR_l361__0ZKy5XK8vhT3cZM
>
< HTTP/1.1 204
< X-Content-Type-Options: nosniff
< X-XSS-Protection: 1; mode=block
< Cache-Control: no-cache, no-store, max-age=0, must-revalidate
< Pragma: no-cache
< Expires: 0
< X-Frame-Options: DENY
< Date: Sun, 03 Apr 2022 07:09:07 GMT
<
* Connection #0 to host localhost left intact
* Closing connection 0
```

The 204 response signifies that the DELETE request is successful, so you have successfully deleted the resource on the server. This can be verified by using the GET call, which will not return any records.

Other HTTP methods can be used in a similar way.

This concludes the basics of cURL commands for API testing via the command prompt. In the next section, you will test the same API endpoints via a GUI using another popular tool.

cURL commands are located at https://github.com/apress/learn-api-testing.

Postman

Postman is an industry-standard GUI tool for developing and testing APIs. It has various advantages, such as sharing the tests with other team members with the help of import/export. Also, a single workplace can be used to develop/share the tests. You can also add authentication, parameterize, and assertions at the collections that can be used by all API tests underneath. In short, you can organize tests in a professional way, and it is much better to use and collaborate with Postman compared to cURL.

You will be using the same set of API endpoints as in the above section for the demonstration of the Postman GUI. You will also learn how to configure a test and have an assertion in place.

Workspace

The workspace is where you have collections (see Figure 4-1). You can create more than one workspace. It is like a project workspace in Eclipse or any other IDE.

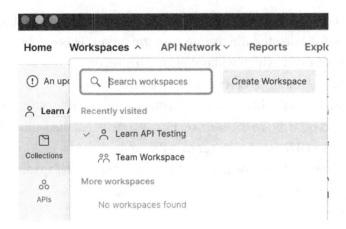

Figure 4-1. *Postman collections*

Globals/Environments

Postman has a concept of global variables (see Figure 4-2) that can be used anywhere in the current workspace. Environment variables can be used in the request call of the API.

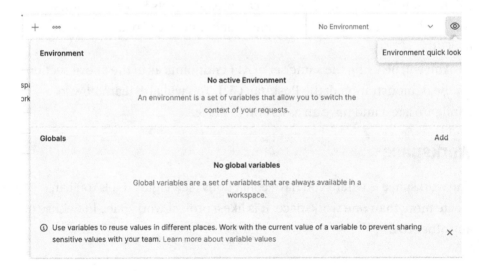

Figure 4-2. *Postman globals and environments*

Collection

Postman collections can help group similar API calls (see Figure 4-3). You can also create folders inside a collection for subgroupings.

Inside a collection, you can use global variables, set authentication, do tests, and perform prerequest scripts. All API calls have access to its collection, and it's up to the API configuration to use it or not.

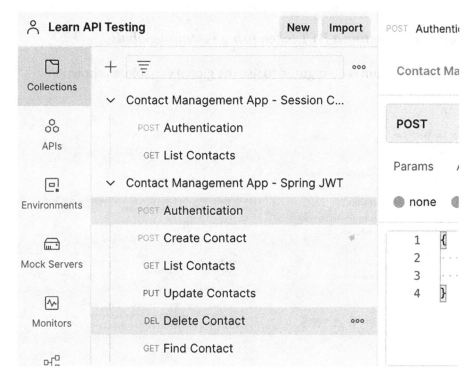

Figure 4-3. *Postman collection*

Authentication

You can set a JWT token as one of the global variables via an `auth/` `authenticate` API call and utilize the same in all API endpoints as the authorization header.

Figure 4-4 shows the script to store the auth_token global variable.

Sales Contact App - Spring JWT / **Authentication**

POST	∨	{{test_url}}/auth/authenticate

Params   Authorization   Headers (9)   Body ●   Pre-request Script   Tests ●   Settings

```
1    var authorization = pm.response.headers.get("Authorization");
2    pm.globals.set("auth_token", authorization);
```

Figure 4-4. *Setting a JWT token using Postman globals*

The collection is configured to use the global variable, as shown in Figure 4-5.

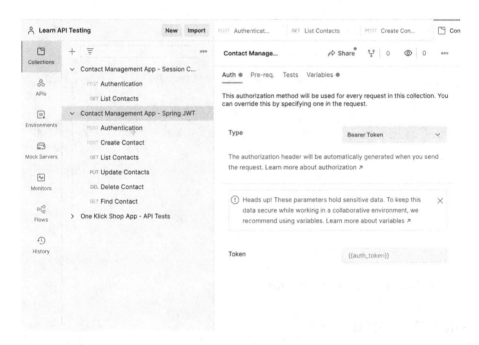

Figure 4-5. *Postman collection configuration*

Parameters

Test parameters can be configured in the collection. Figure 4-6 shows that the `test_url` variable is configured as `http://localhost:8080`.

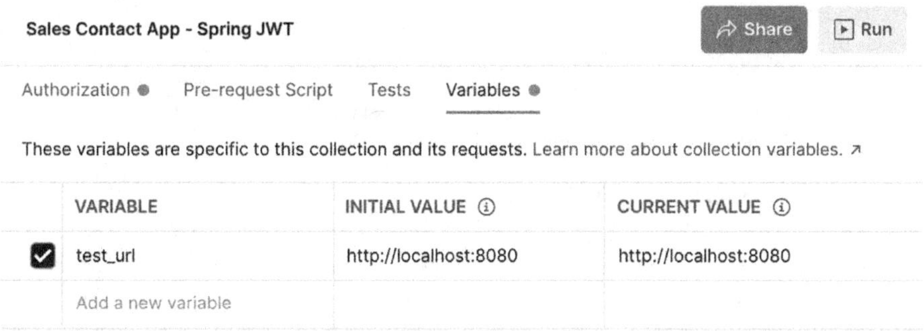

Figure 4-6. *Postman variable configuration*

Assertions

You can have assertions set at the collection level, which will run after every API request. You can also configure additional assertions at the request level.

See line #4 in Figure 4-7 for the assertion code. This is a JavaScript notation.

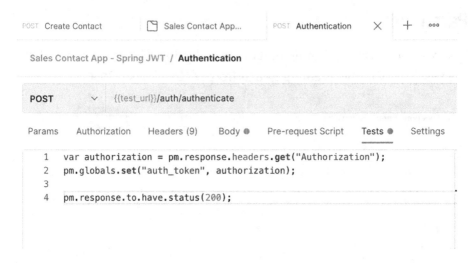

Figure 4-7. Postman assertion

Check the Postman docs for details on test script assertions[1]. Postman tests are located at `https://github.com/apress/learn-api-testing`. You can import this into your workspace before starting the following section. This will help you understand the request quickly.

Requests

A request defines the API endpoint that you want to test. In the Postman GUI, click the three dots on the given collection where you want to create a request and select the Add request menu option. Figure 4-8 shows the navigation to add a new request for a given collection.

---

[1] `https://learning.postman.com/docs/writing-scripts/script-references/test-examples/`

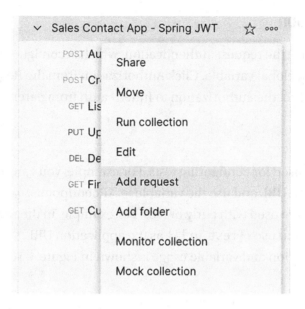

Figure 4-8. *Postman's Add request option*

HTTP Methods

Once the request is created, click the Method drop-down and select the appropriate HTTP method. Figure 4-9 shows the selection of POST as the method type for the given request.

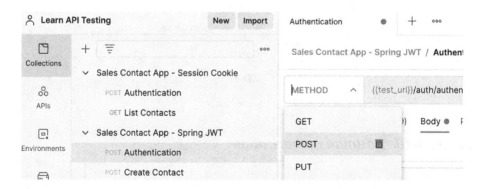

Figure 4-9. *Postman POST request*

Authentication

You need to use the request authentication, which is configured in the collection as a global variable. Click Authorization from the Request submenu and set the authorization to Inherit auth from parent.

Variables

Variables are used for configuring tests. For example, you can configure the test application URL and use the variable in API endpoints.

Variables are used with curly braces. For example, in the request for the POST call, you use {{test_url}} as the application URL.

Authentication and variable usage is shown in Figure 4-10.

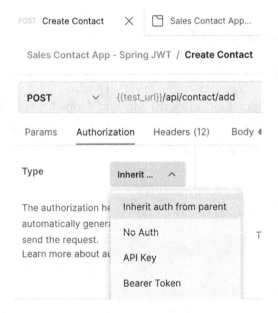

Figure 4-10. *Postman authorization*

Authorization is done using a JWT token. This is set by the `auth/authenticate` call. You need to pass user credentials to get the authorization token from the authorization server. Figure 4-11 shows passing the user credentials to get the authorization token.

You have already seen how to store the authorization token in the global variable `auth_token` in the "Authentication" section. This will set the global variable, and further request calls will use the same variable for authentication.

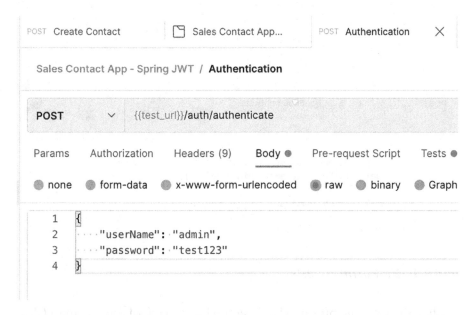

Figure 4-11. *User credentials*

Console

Interactions with requests can be seen in the Postman console. It is good to open the console since it helps in debugging the request.

From the Tests submenu in the request, you can add JavaScript code to print the response as well. The following code snippet can be added to Tests submenu of the `auth/authenticate` call to make sure that the auth_ token global variable is set:

```
console.info(pm.globals.get("auth_token"));
```

Figure 4-12 shows the `auth/authenticate` request in the *Tests* submenu with the above code snippet usage.

Figure 4-12. *Postman tests*

Click the Console button, visible at the bottom left of the Postman GUI, to open the console. Figure 4-13 shows the console.

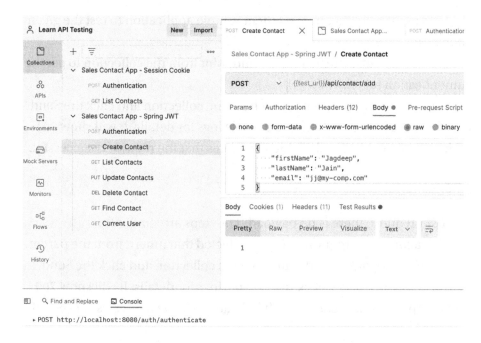

Figure 4-13. Postman console

POST

For a post request, you need to pass in the payload, provide the authorization, and add tests, if any.

1. Click the Body submenu, add the required payload, select raw from the submenu, and select JSON. In the text area, add the payload.

2. Click the Auth submenu and select Inherit from the parent.

3. Click the Tests submenu and add the JavaScript code for the assertion(s).

Let's use the contact management sample application to test the given endpoints.

Trigger the auth/authenticate endpoint from the collection to get the authentication token.

Select Create Contact endpoint from the collection and click the Send button on the request. Check the console logs for details. It will show 201 as the response status code, which indicates that the request is successful.

GET

For a GET request, there is no payload. The steps are similar for authorization for all requests that are selected that inherit from the parent.

Select Find Contact endpoint from the collection and click the Send button on the request. Check the console logs for details. It will show 200 as the response status code, which indicates that the request is successful.

PUT

For a PUT request, add the required payload. Select Update Contact endpoint from the collection and click the Send button on the request. Check the console logs for details. It will show 200 as the response status code, which indicates that the request is successful.

DELETE

For a delete request, there is no payload. Select the Delete Contact endpoint from the collection and click the Send button on the request. Check the console logs for details. It will show 204 as the response status code, which indicates that the contact is deleted. Again, click the find contact; it will show 404 as the response status code, which indicates that the request is having a problem.

Figure 4-14 shows all the requests in the console.

Figure 4-14. *Postman console showing requests*

Postman is a pretty good tool for developers as well as testers while the APIs are in the development stage[2]. In the next section, you will explore RestAssured.

Postman scripts are located at `https://github.com/apress/learn-api-testing`.

RestAssured

RestAssured is an open source REST API testing framework developed and maintained by Johan Haleby[3]. It supports various languages like Java, Kotlin, and Scala. It makes the tester's life easier by allowing them to concentrate on the test rather than worrying about how the request is being served to the server and reading the response from the server. It is a complete package where you can write the code to send requests to the server, read the response from the server, and perform various assertions.

---

[2] `https://learning.postman.com/docs/getting-started/introduction/`
[3] `https://twitter.com/johanhaleby`

RestAssured has its own DSL and works on *give/when/then*. You will exploit its features to write more robust and atomic tests in upcoming chapters.

You'll use RestAssured to do the same operations that you did using cURL and Postman.

Set up a Maven project using the following simple steps:

```
$ mvn archetype:generate -DgroupId=com.contact.mgmt
-DartifactId=restassured-tests -DarchetypeArtifactId=maven-
archetype-quickstart -DarchetypeVersion=1.4
-DinteractiveMode=false
```

Change the directory to the created project and update the pom.xml with the required dependencies. You can overwrite the existing pom.xml with the following code snippet:

```xml
<project xmlns="http://maven.apache.org/POM/4.0.0"
    xmlns:xsi="http://www.w3.org/2001/XMLSchema-instance"
    xsi:schemaLocation="http://maven.apache.org/POM/4.0.0
    http://maven.apache.org/maven-v4_0_0.xsd">
  <modelVersion>4.0.0</modelVersion>
  <groupId>com.contact.mgmt</groupId>
  <artifactId>restassured-tests</artifactId>
  <packaging>jar</packaging>
  <version>1.0-SNAPSHOT</version>
  <name>Contact Management API Test</name>
  <url>http://maven.apache.org</url>
  <properties>
    <maven.test.skip>false</maven.test.skip>
  </properties>
  <dependencies>
    <dependency>
      <groupId>org.junit.jupiter</groupId>
      <artifactId>junit-jupiter-engine</artifactId>
```

```xml
            <version>5.6.2</version>
        </dependency>
        <dependency>
            <groupId>org.junit.vintage</groupId>
            <artifactId>junit-vintage-engine</artifactId>
            <version>5.6.2</version>
        </dependency>
        <dependency>
            <groupId>io.rest-assured</groupId>
            <artifactId>rest-assured</artifactId>
            <version>4.5.0</version>
            <scope>test</scope>
        </dependency>
    </dependencies>
    <build>
        <plugins>
            <plugin>
                <artifactId>maven-compiler-plugin</artifactId>
                <version>3.8.1</version>
                <configuration>
                    <source>1.8</source>
                    <target>1.8</target>
                </configuration>
            </plugin>
            <plugin>
                <artifactId>maven-surefire-plugin</artifactId>
                <version>2.22.2</version>
            </plugin>
        </plugins>
    </build>
</project>
```

Highlighted is the RestAssured dependency.

Create a test class as `ContactManagementTest.java`.

Define the variable as follows. This is the application URL under test.

```
private final String app = "http://localhost:8080/app";
```

To get the authorization token, add the following method in the test class:

```java
private String getJwtToken() {
 String admin = "src/test/resources/admin.json";
 String url = app + "/auth/authenticate";
 return
     given()
     .body(new File(admin))
     .contentType("application/json")
     .when()
     .post(url).getHeader("Authorization");
}
```

`admin` variable is the authentication payload.

`post(url).getHeader("Authorization");` http POST method reads the token from the response and returns to the caller

Let's add test methods for `Create`, `Find`, `Update`, and `Delete`.

Add the following code snippet for `Create Contact`:

```java
@Test
@DisplayName("Create Contact")
public void tesAddContact() {
 String addContact = "src/test/resources/contact.json";
 String url = app + "/api/v1/contacts";
 given()
```

```
        .body(new File(addContact))
        .header("Authorization", "Bearer " + getJwtToken())
        .contentType("application/json")
        .when()
        .post(url)
        .then()
        .statusCode(201);
}
```

addContact is the request payload with details of the contact that you need to create:

```
String url = app + "/api/v1/contacts"; this is the endpoint for
creating contact
```

```
post(url) this is the http POST method
```

```
then().statusCode(201); does the assertion on the response
status code
```

Add the following code snippet for Update Contact:

```
@Test
@DisplayName("Update Contact")
public void tesUpdateContact() {
 String updateContact = "src/test/resources/
 updateContact.json";
 String url = app + "/api/v1/contacts/{id}";
 HashMap<String, Integer> query = new HashMap<>();
 query.put("id", 1001);
 given()
      .body(new File(updateContact))
      .header("Authorization", "Bearer " + getJwtToken())
      .contentType("application/json")
```

```
.when()
.put(url, query)
.then()
.statusCode(200);
```

updateContact is the request payload with the details of the contact that you need to update:

```
String url = app + "/api/v1/contacts/{id}"; this is the
endpoint for updating contact
```

```
query.put("id", 1001); this will be used for passing the query
parameter
```

```
put(url, query) this is the http PUT method
```

```
then().statusCode(200); does the assertion on the response
status code
```

Add the following code snippet for Find Contact:

```
@Test
@DisplayName("Find Contact")
public void tesFindContact() {
 String url = app + "/api/v1/contacts/{id}";
 HashMap<String, Integer> query = new HashMap<>();
 query.put("id",1002);
 given()
     .header("Authorization", "Bearer " + getJwtToken())
     .contentType("application/json")
     .when()
     .get(url, query)
     .then()
     .statusCode(200);
}
```

String url = app + "/api/v1/contacts/{id}"; this is the endpoint for find the contact

query.put("id",1002); this will be used for passing the query parameter

get(url, query) this is the http GET method

then().statusCode(200); does the assertion on the response status code

Add the following code snippet for Find Contact:

```
@Test
@DisplayName("Delete Contact")
public void tesDeleteContact() {
 String url = app + "/api/v1/contacts/{id}";
 HashMap<String, Integer> query = new HashMap<>();
 query.put("id", 1003);
 given()
     .header("Authorization", "Bearer " + getJwtToken())
     .contentType("application/json")
     .when()
     .delete(url, query)
     .then()
     .statusCode(204);
}
```

String url = app + "/api/v1/contacts/{id}"; this will be used for passing the query parameter

query.put("id", 1003); this will be used for passing the query parameter

```
delete(url, query) this is the http DELETE method
```

```
then().statusCode(204); does the assertion on the response
status code
```

Let's execute the test. Enter the following command in the terminal window:

```
$ mvn clean test
```

Test execution results will be as shown below.

```
[INFO] Scanning for projects...
.
[INFO] Building Contact Management API Test 1.0-SNAPSHOT
.
[INFO]  T E S T S
[INFO] com.contact.mgmt.api.tests.ContactManagementTest
[INFO] Tests run: 4, Failures: 0, Errors: 0, Skipped: 0, Time
        elapsed: 3.849 s - in com.contact.mgmt.api.tests.
        ContactManagementTest
[INFO]
[INFO] Results:
[INFO]
[INFO] Tests run: 4, Failures: 0, Errors: 0, Skipped: 0
[INFO]
[INFO] ------------------------------------------------------------
[INFO] BUILD SUCCESS
[INFO] ------------------------------------------------------------
[INFO] Total time: 7.547 s
[INFO] Finished at: 2022-04-03T14:37:58+05:30
[INFO] Final Memory: 18M/211M
[INFO] ------------------------------------------------------------
```

You can see that all the tests passed.

This is the simplest way to write RestAssured-based API tests. In Chapter 9 and 10, you will develop a test framework from scratch and will write atomic tests built upon the RestAssured framework.

The RestAssured project is located at `https://github.com/apress/learn-api-testing`.

Frameworks/Libraries

A standard test script has a test method and a logger for the steps and errors. The output is stored in some data structure for assertions at the end of the script. Also, the test script is configurable to run on any test environment. This section is just to get an overview of these frameworks/libraries. In later chapters, when you develop a framework, you will explore these frameworks/libraries more.

If you are not aware of these frameworks/libraries, please go through the respective docs on the usage.

TestNG

Writing test automation requires a framework, which helps in formalizing the test script. TestNG is a framework that is used quite widely in the software testing community.

JUnit is the unit testing framework that is quite popular among Java developers for unit testing. TestNG has adapted the JUnit style of writing tests and has very good support in the open source community.

TestNG has its own advantages, like creating a test suite using XML-based document, annotations, parallel test execution, data providers, and a few more features that make it a good choice as a test framework.

You will be using TestNG to write API tests. You will go over a few features in upcoming chapters when you start writing test scripts.

You can learn more about TestNG at `https://testng.org/doc/`.

Log4j

Test scripts need logging, just like the software source code. Log4j is a popular library for logging steps as well as exceptions during test execution. It is a good way to debug tests. You will be using this library in the test framework.

Log4j is an XML document in which you define how the test script logs the text based on the context and log level like INFO, WARN, or ERROR.

Due to recent log4j vulnerability, please go through the log4j doc[4] to find the suitable version to use in the test framework.

Jackson-Databind[5]

The API returns JSON, and as a tester you need to parse the response for assertions. One of the best JSON-to-Java libraries is Jackson-Databind. You will be using this in the test framework to store the API response for ease of use and better readability. Needless to say, assertj does a pretty good job in asserting Java objects.

HashMap

A few APIs require parameters in the URL. With the help of HashMap, you can parameterize the API. HashMap[6] is a Java collection that you will be using in the test framework.

---

[4] `https://logging.apache.org/log4j/2.x/`
[5] `https://github.com/FasterXML/jackson-databind`
[6] `https://docs.oracle.com/javase/8/docs/api/java/util/HashMap.html`

Assertj

Every test needs assertions. Although test assertions are provided by TestNG, assertj is the most convenient because of its easy-to-use methods plus a variety of assertions support, which includes Java collections.

Next, you will be learning what to use from assertj. Meanwhile, you should go through the documentation at `https://assertj.github.io/doc/`.

Java Spring

Java Spring has one of the best frameworks. It's removed a lot of boilerplate code and has packages at your disposal for configuring out how tests can be executed.

You will be using the Java Spring `@Configuration`, `@PropertySource`, and `@ComponentScan` annotations and Spring Bean to configure API tests as well as test environments. You will see the usage in the later chapters.

Summary

In this chapter, you learned about standard tools for testing APIs of software applications. Also, you went through useful frameworks and libraries, which you will be using in the upcoming chapters. In the next chapter, you will learn about the test pyramid.

CHAPTER 5

Test Pyramid

In the previous chapter, you learned about the tools, frameworks, and libraries used for automation testing. This chapter introduces the test pyramid and why it's crucial to visualize tests on each layer of a software application.

At the end of this chapter, you should have a good idea about the importance of a layered testing approach and how it helps save time and effort.

Mike Cohn[1] created a test pyramid[2] that offers a practical way of testing software applications. This was before the agile methodology came into existence. Later, Martin Fowler[3] mentioned the test pyramid in terms of agile testing in his blog about the test pyramid[4].

For a software development team, it is important to understand the necessity of testing for customer success. For a typical software application, we can define testing efforts using a test pyramid. The test pyramid also helps in identifying the layer where testing is needed the most. It helps save time and effort. This concept is time-tested; it's a practical approach towards testing. Software should fail early and fail fast. If this is not the case, then either the code is not buggy or we need to write more tests to break it.

---

[1] https://en.wikipedia.org/wiki/Mike_Cohn
[2] www.mountaingoatsoftware.com/blog/the-forgotten-layer-of-the-test-automation-pyramid
[3] https://en.wikipedia.org/wiki/Martin_Fowler_(software_engineer)
[4] https://martinfowler.com/bliki/TestPyramid.html

© Jagdeep Jain 2022
J. Jain, *Learn API Testing*, https://doi.org/10.1007/978-1-4842-8142-0_5

In a typical software development team, developers test their own code and then a code review meeting is set up where the architect or the lead is assigned to review the code. Once the code is ready for testing, the testers start testing the software application.

Before getting into the test pyramid, let's go through what happens on a regular day-to-day software development team. Developers deliver the code with the unit test coverage. A CI/CD pipeline is set up where all the unit tests are executed before the testers start testing the functionality. Front-end testers write the functional test plan and test the GUI. Back-end testers write the middle tier test plan, which cover the business components and communication between them, which are basically the services.

The above testing activities can be categorized into black box, gray box, and white box testing.

Black Box Testing

Testers who test an application like an end user, without knowing any internal details about the software, are termed *black box testers* and their activity is termed *black box testing*.

These testers follow the functional requirements given by the end user, and the goal is to check whether all the given functional requirements are working as expected. They enter the input and expect the output to be bound to some condition(s) without knowing how the application internally processes the request and sends the response.

This type of testing is usually performed at the GUI level.

Testing each of the workflows is time-consuming and usually takes weeks if not days. Testers may write automated test scripts to save time and resources.

Do not confuse this with UAT testing or beta testing. Black box testing is performed by testers or those who are supposed to use the product. This is usually done before the production release.

Grey Box Testing

Testers who are aware of the customer requirements as well as the internal working of the software application perform what is called *grey box testing*. This usually involves testing the internal communication between the components as well as confirming whether unknown conditions are handled well by the system. An example of an unknown condition is when a user enters an invalid input or a data type that is not compatible, the application should throw the correct exception/error message. It is crucial to test all component interactions and services thoroughly because any miss may result in software malfunction.

White Box Testing

White box testing covers code paths, checks complexity of the code, and so on. In short, white box testing checks whether the developer uses the right algorithm or not. Unit testing is a subset of white box testing where the developer knows the technical details of the system as well as the functional requirements of the software application.

In the competitive market, software development has evolved and so has software testing. Software testing is not just finding bugs, but also finding bugs as early as possible and hitting the layer where there is more possibility of bugs. At the same time, we need to save time and money. This is where the test pyramid helps in finding the balance in testing.

Test Pyramid

If you have already set up and are running test automation, draw the triangle. If the triangle matches what is shown in Figure 5-1, then you are already following the test pyramid. But if the number of GUI tests are more than the unit tests or API tests, then it is quite certain that testing time is longer, the tests are often flaky, and the testers' time goes into finding script issues vs. bugs.

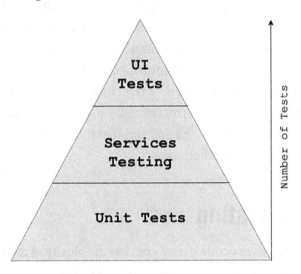

Figure 5-1. *The test pyramid*

There are various GUI test automation tools that can be used for test automation. If you have already experienced GUI automation, then probably you have also seen that GUI automation tests take a lot more time to write and the test execution cycles are longer. Usually the ratio is 1:5 (varies depending upon complexity of the software application). That is, the time to write a single GUI test is equal to time to write five API tests. Also, the execution of services tests is much faster (provided the API is performance-tuned).

The test pyramid says that testers should invest more time in testing the middle layer than the GUI layer. We will skip the unit testing part for now since this book is more about learning API tests.

The tester's objective is to find more bugs in less time. Based on experience, GUI testing takes more time in test development and execution compared to API testing. We can test all permutations and combinations of the business logic at the API layer. GUI testing is end-to-end testing and does not involve how the internal components work together.

The cost of finding a bug at the API layer is much lower and the effort in finding the bug is less compared to GUI layer testing. Computation and data testing must be taken care of at the services layer; it's difficult and time-consuming to do so on the GUI layer.

The rule of thumb is *do not repeat the test if it is already covered in the layer below.*

Non-functional testing, like performance, security, and such, should be done on the services layer. On the GUI layer, tests should be limited to front-end security testing.

Summary

In this chapter, you went through the test categories and learned about the test pyramid. You also learned that testing at the top layer should be minimal and the bottom layer should have the maximum number of tests. Also, you now know that repeating a test is not a good idea. In the next chapter, you will learn about what needs to be tested at the API layer.

CHAPTER 6

Testing the API

In earlier chapters, you learned why we need API testing and the advantages of doing so. You also learned about web application architecture, the HTTP protocol, and various authentication techniques. This chapter will walk you through the aspects of API testing—the API testing paradigm.

At the end of this chapter, you should have a good knowledge about what things must be tested on a given API. You will also know some keywords that are commonly used in the industry.

A typical API requires the HTTP protocol and has a payload, a request, and response as well as a request header and response header. You have learned various aspects of web application architecture, HTTP protocol, and authentication for requesting a resource. Let's dive into specifics and find out what you need to test as a part of API testing.

Note that since we all now do iterative development, testing is a part of the development team (not like the waterfall model). Testing should be faster and able to find bugs, as you learned in the last chapter on the test pyramid. If you define test standards, or a set of rules, or a checklist on the hows and whats of API testing, it will be much easier to write test automation, find more bugs, and then improvise. With this in mind, let's continue our discussion on the API testing paradigm.

© Jagdeep Jain 2022
J. Jain, *Learn API Testing*, https://doi.org/10.1007/978-1-4842-8142-0_6

Workflows/Use Cases/Test Script

The product owner provides workflows and use cases to the development team. The workflow defines what the system is supposed to do. The use case is the interaction of a user with the system.

Typical workflow examples are taking orders, making payments, shipping orders, and so on.

A use case is the steps a user performs while placing the order. It may involve touching most of the workflows or maybe just one.

Testers review the workflows and use cases. Before starting test automation, they write test scripts in the format agreed upon by the team (in most of the cases, it is a spreadsheet). The agreed-upon format helps the team in the review process.

Writing elaborated test scripts is useful for writing test automation.

For API testing, you need to add details like input data, datatype, and the format of the request. You also need to add expected results in the test script, like what data is expected, in what format, the response format, and such. This is crucial for the UI developer because they use the API to show data on the UI based on the user request.

The API has a request/response schema (XML or JSON), which in turn has a request parameter and response values. You need to test the schema, data, and the data type. You also need other factors, which we will discuss in the sections below.

Schema Validation

As a part of schema testing, you must make sure that the schema is correct and based on the requirements. API details are usually part of the documentation. It gives all the details about the request/response body and the data types. We will discuss the API documentation in later chapters.

A JSON schema can be created with the help of online tools or manually based on experience. You can choose the manner as per your need; however, a two good options are `https://jsonschema.net/` and `https://jsonformatter.org/json-to-jsonschema` .

A sample schema of a contact management application generated by `https://jsonformatter.org/json-to-jsonschema` is as follows:

```
{
    "$schema": "http://json-schema.org/draft-06/schema#",
    "type": "array",
    "items": {
        "$ref": "#/definitions/contactManagement"
    },
    "definitions": {
        "contactManagement": {
            "type": "object",
            "additionalProperties": false,
            "properties": {
                "id": {
                    "type": "integer"
                },
                "firstName": {
                    "type": "string"
                },
                "lastName": {
                    "type": "string"
                },
                "email": {
                    "type": "string"
                }
            },
            "required": [
```

```
            "email",
            "firstName",
            "id",
            "lastName"
        ],
        "title": "contactManagement"
      }
   }
};
```

Schema validation consists of the following:

- The data type matches with the requirements.

- The required/mandatory parameters are present.

- The type of schema is correct (JSON Object or JSON Array).

With the help of Postman, you can test the JSON schema. Let's see the Postman code snippet in the Tests submenu:

```
var jsonResponse = pm.response.json();
var salesAppSchema = <this will be the schema, same as given in
above sample schema>

pm.test('schema is valid', function() {
    pm.expect(tv4.validate(jsonResponse,salesAppSchema)).
    to.be.true;
});
```

Hit the request and the test will validate the schema. Figure 6-1 shows that the schema test is a PASS.

Figure 6-1. *JSON schema validation*

Postman scripts can be downloaded from `https://github.com/Apress/Learn-API-Testing`.

Test Coverage

API test coverage is said to be good if it covers all functional aspects of the software application, the technical aspects of the API, versioning, error logging, request and response headers, request and response parameters, the data including invalid data and data injection (and few other aspects of security testing), and finally the performance. It's good to have the testing API documented if the APIs are exposed to the external world.

Header Testing

Header testing is an important part of API testing since it has the metadata information, authorization token, the content type information, the expiry of the token, and many more aspects that are crucial for the API to work efficiently.

Request Header

Request headers play a major role in making sure that API works as per the technical and functional aspects.

Request headers can be exploited by a hacker, so it is very important from the security testing perspective. Since we are talking about functional testing, we will discuss a few important things about the request headers. Feel free to explore more ways based on the domain or software application you are testing.

Correct Header

First thing first, you need to make sure that passing correct headers does work.

Missing Header

Do not pass the required headers and check the API response. The response should be 4XX, a malformed request. For example, do not pass the content-type, authorization header, required media type, or compression format.

Incorrect Header

Pass incorrect headers (like, for a JSON payload, pass text-html) and check the API response. The response should indicated that the header is not correct.

Use a malformed/expired authorization token to gain access to the API resource. The response should tell the user that the token is malformed.

For an OAuth2 token, check whitelisted redirects.

Unsupported Type

For a media application, you can pass unsupported media types and check if they are understood by the API. The response should show an appropriate error message.

Response Header

Response headers are crucial for the success of the API. The following sections cover a few examples.

Supported Type

The content-type in the response header should be based on the schema used for API development.

If it's a media application, the supported media type should be given in the response.

Response Codes

For a successful response, the response code should be 200. For an authorization call from the authentication server, the response code should be 301. Find similar examples for the application under test and add a few tests around the response code. This becomes more crucial when the APIs are exposed to the external world; as such, a small mistake may lead to loss of business.

Request Body

Testing the request body has a lot of scope if everything is set up correctly, such as the metadata in the headers. But if the request body is not correct and is missed in testing, it directly impacts the functionality of the application. Let's check what can be tested as a part of the request body.

Format Unsupported

Send a text format as a payload and check the response. Only supported formats should be allowed by the API.

Special Characters

Send special characters in the payload in place of the string data type and check the API response. Some foreign languages have special characters that should be supported in case the API supports all locales.

Very Long Strings

For a name or any other string, pass in a very long string in the payload and check the API response. The API should not allow a string that is greater than the column size in the database.

CHAPTER 6   TESTING THE API

Invalid Method

Use POST instead of PUT and check if the API responds to the request. The API should throw an error if the endpoint does not have the required access method, which is given in the API documentation,

Invalid Value

For integers values, pass in decimal values. For Boolean values, pass in a string like "true" (in quotes). You can be more creative in finding issues since all these values will end up in the database at the end of the day if the operation is adding the values to the database, such as contact information.

Incorrect Data Type

Instead of integers, pass in string values and check the API response. The API should throw an error appropriately.

Empty Data/Object

Pass in an empty JSON object as a payload and check the response. Also, pass in an empty string to check the API response. The API should not allow these inputs. Empty strings will ultimately end up in the database if the operation is adding new data.

Required Fields

Remove the required fields from the payload and check the API response. The API should show appropriate error messages if the required fields are missing.

Null

Send null as values in the payload and check the response. The API should show appropriate error messages.

Redundant Fields

Pass in redundant fields, such as fields that are not required. Also, pass additional fields that are not in the definition of the payload and check the response. The API should not allow additional fields. The redundant fields, if not in the definition, should not be allowed.

DELETE Already Deleted Entity

This is more specific to the DELETE method. Once the entry is deleted from the database, hit the same API again and check the response. The API should respond with a message that the entity does not exist. This is more of an implementation detail that you need to check for the DELETE endpoint.

Duplicate Check

For add operation, you should check if the duplicate check is enabled on the API endpoint or not, based on the business requirements. For example, the email ID and the phone number should be unique for contacts.

You also need to check if the update operation is duplicating the record in the database.

Response Body

The response body is the validation of the expected data based on the input, which is called the *actual data*. A response can be big in size as well, so you need to make sure that it is handled properly by the given API.

Actual Data vs. Expected Data

Let's say you are requesting a list of contacts. The response would be having the list of contacts with the fields based on the API definition.

Limit/Size/Pagination/Sorting

You need to make sure that the API returns the data in the specified format. There is also pagination. The size of the response should also be checked since it directly impacts the performance of the API.

API Version Testing

This category contains backward-compatibility tests. If the endpoint changes, the old one should not be removed, but when the user hits the old endpoint, it should redirect to the new endpoint.

Internal vs. External APIs

APIs that are not accessible to the external world are called internal APIs. As a part of the standard testing practice, you need to make sure that the internal APIs are not accessible by the outside world. There should be an IP whitelisting of the internal APIs, those outside the list, and the APIs that are inaccessible.

APIs that are exposed to the external world ought to be consistent, secure, and scalable based on the high usage. It is also good to monitor the external API, find out the usage patterns, and draw up testing guidelines accordingly. For example, if the external world is frequently fetching the list of contacts, then you need to make sure that the performance of the API is good enough. And if the external world is interested in deleting something, then the copy of the data must be preserved or not, based on the geo location laws.

The definition of the external API should never change; that is, the tests should never fail in ideal conditions. But if they fail, it will be P0 and must be fixed immediately. You can also pick up beta testers from the API consumers and ask them to help with test reviews.

For external APIs, security testing should include tests for SQL injection, remote code execution, and such.

Consumer-Driven Contract Testing

CDCT applies to external APIs. They are often services offered by vendors to the external world, like weather or currency conversion. The definition of the API becomes the contract, and the consumer drives the testing of these APIs. Consumers add the test automation and share the same with the vendor. The vendor, in turn, runs these tests as a part of CI/CD pipeline, and any red flag is taken seriously and must be fixed in a few hours, if not minutes.

Importance of Negative Testing

Negative testing is a very important part of API testing since it exposes weaknesses in the API implementation. It is suggested to do enough negative testing so that you get a clean user interaction and the user is not allowed to push garbage data into the application. Negative testing helps identify bugs that may crash the application. For example, in a file upload API, if the size limit is not set, then the user may upload a large file, which may end up crashing the application server. Another example is a shopping cart application that is allowed to set the product cost to zero. Negative testing is particularly significant for domains such as banking, finance, and insurance where, if not done, the business may end up having varied legal issues with customers. Discussion of the testing approach is out of the scope of this book, but the tester should be diligent in finding all scenarios that may be a threat to the business.

API testing should be done thoroughly since it impacts the overall application, both the front end and the back end. In the event of poor API testing, the back end will have garbage data, which is not useful. If the response to the user input was not tested well enough, the front end will have issues if the user makes a mistake, intentionally passes invalid values, or enters garbage data.

Summary

In this chapter, you learned what needs to be tested at the API layer, including the headers, requests, and responses. You also learned about negative testing, internal vs. external APIs, and consumer-driven contract testing. In the next chapter, you will examine a good test script.

CHAPTER 7

A Good Test Script

In the earlier chapters, you developed an understanding of API testing, web application architecture, token-based authentication, tools, frameworks, libraries, and the test pyramid. In the previous chapter, you learned what to test on a given API. In this chapter, you will learn about the components of a good test script and the guidelines for a good test script.

At the end of this chapter, you'll know what a good test script should contain and the guidelines for writing a good and readable test script. These guidelines will help in code reviews and save a lot of time between the software developer and the reviewer.

For a software developer, it is crucial to write good code so that it can be reviewed easily, can debug faster, and any new changes can be accommodated quickly. At the same time, it should be less complex, take less memory, and be faster to execute.

For a software tester, the test script should be readable, execute faster, take less memory, have similar steps as the user interactions, and be easy to review.

Before starting a test framework, it is good to define the components of a test script and the set of guidelines that should be followed to write an efficient test script that has all the characteristics of a good test script. This will help in code reviews and speed up the writing of test scripts.

Let's discuss the components of a good test script and the guidelines that you may find to be a good fit for any project. It is always better to set the guidelines in advance to make sure that they evolve as you get closer to completing the test automation. They can be agreed upon during team meetings.

© Jagdeep Jain 2022
J. Jain, *Learn API Testing*, https://doi.org/10.1007/978-1-4842-8142-0_7

Components of a Test Script

Test scripts can be thought of as steps that are applied to make sure that the product under test is as per the standard guidelines of the industry. If the test script does not find any issues, it is assumed that the product is QA certified and okay to be used by end users.

Before starting to test the product, you must make sure that product is available and is configured as per the test requirements. Once you know you have the right configuration, follow the steps to make sure that the product under the given configuration works well. Based on the outcome, you can decide that the product in the given configuration is good, as per the expected outcome, and is good for user testing or not. Once the configuration is tested, you need to reset the product to a different configuration.

This is applied to all types of testing, from software testing to hardware testing. Based on this, you can deduce the required components of a test script.

```
setup() {
  // configure the product
}

test() {
  // test steps
  // test outcome validation
}

teardown() {
  // reset the configuration
}
```

setup()

For a software web application, setup sets up the application configuration like the application URL, user credentials, user role, and so on.

test()

The test step involves the use case or the workflow (for any user), and the test outcome validation is the assertion that the tester will be doing to make sure that the test is successful or failed.

For API testing, the test script should be the same as the actual calls. For example, if you are creating a contact, then the test script should be two lines max. The first is a call to an API endpoint like post(endpoint, payload); and the next line asserts the response.

Check out the following example:

```
testCreateContact() {
  post(endpoint, payload);
  assertThat(actualResponse).isEqualTo(expectedResponse);
}
```

This is the simplest and best example of a good test script. The framework should support boilerplate code so that the test script is very short, meaningful, and readable.

teardown()

The tear down step cleans up the test configuration, invalidates the session, and more.

Don't add lines of code in tearDown() that will delete something to clean up the database. Discuss better options with the team because the test script is meant for testing stuff, not for cleaning up databases.

For a good test script, the components should not be more than what is absolutely required. It has to be simple with a minimal number of lines of code. Making it complex increases the debugging time and it is difficult to maintain.

Guidelines

Having a set of guidelines is good for maintaining the standard of test automation, and at the same time it gives you an opportunity to improvise. The following sections offer guidelines for writing good test automation scripts. These guidelines are standard and can be applied to UI testing (a UI test script should have an additional set of guidelines since it deals with browser DOM elements), API testing, or any other testing layer you may want to apply.

Single-Attempt Test

Avoid writing and pushing (pushing to code repository) a test multiple times. It should be pushed to the repository only when it is self-reviewed based on the guidelines and coding standards. (We will discuss coding guidelines in the next chapter.)

This improves your confidence and habit of writing code in a single attempt. It also helps code reviews.

Document Test Objective

Use the TestNG @Test annotation with the `description` tag (or any other tool if it supports the documentation, or it can be under comments as well). The test description should be as small as possible and convey the meaning of the test.

Look at the following line of code:

```
@Test (description = "Verify adding a contact is successful.")
```

Keep It Small

A test script should be written for a single objective. It should be named accordingly.

Do not mix different types of assertions in a single test. Otherwise, if one of the assertions fails, it will be assumed that the test failed, even if all the remaining assertions pass. Having a single assertion, on the other hand, isolates the issues and thus helps find issues faster.

Test only one part of the API at a time, or one functionality at a time, if the API has few additional things to do (ideally, this will not be a case with microservices). For example, check the headers in a different test, and the response in another; test schema in one test and the body in another test.

Use assertj for Assertions

You learned about assertj in Chapter 4. You should use the industry's best assertion library because it covers a wide range of responses.

assertj is one of the best libraries for assertions in Java-based test frameworks. It has fluent assertion support that increases readability.

Consider the following example:

```
LinkedList<String> expectedContactColumnName
        = new LinkedList<>(
          Arrays.asList(
            "FIRST NAME",
            "SECOND NAME",
            "EMAIL",
            "CONTACT NUMBER"
```

```
        )
    );
```

assertThat(contact.getContactColumnName()).**isEqualTo(expected**
ContactColumnName);

Note   Do not mix assertion libraries like TestNG and JUnit. Use only assertj.

Use log4j

You learned about log4j in Chapter 4. You can use log4j for better logging practices. Let's say you need to create a report of what tests were executed, the steps, and that the test failures were logged appropriately, which in turn conveys the failure messages.

Consider the following example:

```
log.info("Test [{}] \n Steps: \n [{}]", description, steps);
```

Note   Do not use System.out.println()because it slows down the overall test execution.

Order of Tests

You should not have the order of tests defined in the test script or test framework. If the first test fails, the dependent tests are skipped or assumed to be failed since the precondition does not meet expectations.

The objective of testing is to find the bug in the software application as early as possible, which is not possible if you make the process complex in order to shorten the test script efforts.

It is always better to have a single test per test class. Avoid a test framework like the following:

```
public class ContactCRUDTest {
  public void createContactTest () {
    // create contact
      assertThat(response).equals(200);
  }

  public void updateContactTest () {
    // update the above contact
        assertThat(response).equals(200);
  }
}
```

This is a CRUD test class in which you are creating a contact first and then updating the same. This means that if the create contact fails, the update contact is skipped. You don't want this since it is just that create contact is not working, but the update contact might be working.

No Interventions Between Test Steps

It is a common practice to connect with the database and make assertions. You should avoid doing multiple things in the test script.

A test script is a set of user steps. The user inputs something and expects something out of it. The user does not connect with the database or any other third-party system. It is the job of the API to do all these things, or some background process that runs based on the API call and provides results to the API.

It is good to avoid the highlighted code:

```
public class ContactListTest {
  public void contactListTest () {
    login();
    // some steps here
    assertThat(actualResult).equals(expectedResult);
    connect.db().getValues();
    assertThat(value1).equals.equals(value2);
    connect.shell().retrieveValues();
    logout();
  }
}
```

Do not connect with the database between the test, or any other system like the shell, as this is not efficient testing. Connecting to the database and retrieving results after the API call will drain down the total execution time; if the database password changes, your test will fail. The same goes with connecting to shells.

Avoid Hard Sleeps

Sometimes the API response is too slow during the development cycle and the developer is engaged in fixing the API response time. During this time, it is tempting to add the delay in the test script before the assertion. You should not do this at any cost. First, because you would not know whether the response time is fixed or not and you may forget to remove the sleep time. Second, it impacts the overall test execution time.

Avoid `Thread.sleep();`

Always Use Assertions

Recall components of tests from the above sections of this chapter. Test script should have at least one assertion. Without an assertion, a test is not really a test but a set of steps that get executed without any objective.

Testing is all about finding a bug. Without an assertion, there is no meaning to testing.

Do Not Overtest

Always write tests that have a possibility of finding the bug. Test the happy path first and then do negative testing. Think about the user before writing any test scripts. Extra tests will result in more time to execute the tests and also take time and resources for test maintenance.

Do Not Import a Test into Another Test

There is a possibility of similar code in almost all tests. For example, assertions are similar in a couple of tests. Assertions are a part of a test script. It may be that the same assertions are being used for other tests. Assertions are an integral part of the test script. Always have individual assertions for each test; if not, you'll need to debug the issue if the test fails. Also, you will end up in code manipulation and writing various if-then conditions. So, it is best to have individual test assertions.

Do not write helper functions in the test class, such as getting the current time in milliseconds, or the same set of assertions that are being used in other test classes. Always use the standard helper class and import it in your base test.

It may seem convenient to call one test method in another test, but you should avoid doing this. The test class is meant to have test methods run as a part of the test execution.

Test Boundaries

It is important to understand the test boundaries. Discuss them within the team and find out what you should not test. Without finalizing the test boundaries, you will end up writing tests that may not be required or have no impact. This will increase overall test execution time.

Testers should be good in utilizing CPU time and the memory footprint.

API Test Coverage

Make sure that the API test coverage includes user roles and permissions. You are testing external APIs as per guidelines/contract. Always check data types and values like string vs. integer, null vs. zero, or empty values in the response.

Test individual APIs. Also form an end-to-end test and combine several APIs. If similar data is present as a response in several other APIs, compare the data in the given APIs. There is a high chance that you will find a regression.

Provide Short Commands

Utilize the power of Maven and configure test suites in `pom.xml`. Provide team members short commands for executing tests. Use Maven Profiles to create the test suite. It's like writing a CLI (command line) application.

```
<profile>
   <!-- end to end test suite -->
   <id>e2e</id>
```

Do not `try{} catch{}`

Do not catch `AssertErrors` or any other exception inside the test script. It may be the case that you are missing the actual behavior of the API.

Summary

In this chapter, you learned the components of a good test script as well as the guidelines to follow while writing a good test script. In the next chapter, you will learn about coding guidelines.

CHAPTER 8

Coding Guidelines

To continue the previous chapter, in this chapter you will get to know coding guidelines to follow in order to write a good and readable test script, as well as a few coding best practices for the test framework.

This chapter will make you aware of the things that are widely missed and never perceived later in the project life cycle, but if used will make test automation much better and joyful. This chapter is influenced by various learnings during office hours by looking at each other's code and finding flaws.

At the end of this chapter, you should know how to write good code that is readable. When implementing best practices at the workplace, these guidelines will help in code reviews and save a lot of time between the test development engineer and the reviewer.

Coding best practices and guidelines can also be agreed upon in a team meeting. The information in the following sections will be a good fit for any project.

Coding best practices apply to test classes as well as supporting code, which enables the test to be clean and readable.

Coding Best Practices

A test framework evolves with each development project. Some organizations have developed their own standard test framework, which must be used by all development teams. Other teams develop the

© Jagdeep Jain 2022
J. Jain, *Learn API Testing*, https://doi.org/10.1007/978-1-4842-8142-0_8

framework as per the needs of the development project. Each approach has advantages and disadvantages.

Developing a framework for the organization has its own challenges, whereas developing a custom framework for a team is easier to manage. For a custom framework, changes can be made easily when few teams depend on the base classes. With a standard framework, making any changes in the base class requires approvals from all teams, and if anything breaks, then a delay in release is inevitable.

While you consider using a standard test framework or a custom framework for a specific team/project, it is really important to follow coding best practices so that anyone inside or outside the team has no problem using the base classes.

Every organization has standard coding practices for projects. The code review committee makes you follow the guidelines. But it's the duty of the software engineer to write better code. Apart from standard coding best practices, there are few more things that need to be considered if you are developing an API testing framework.

Let's discuss a few of the coding best practices for an API testing framework. They may apply to a UI testing framework as well as any other testing framework.

Class Naming Conventions

A class name should always be singular. The name depicts the object in accordance with OOP principles. For example, if you are storing a contact, the name of the class should be Contact but not Contacts. The class name should convey the exact purpose based on the requirements.

Method Naming Conventions

Follow the camelCase rule. Keep it simple and straightforward. For HTTP methods, name them as get(), post(), put(), delete(), and so on. They will be called from the test script. The objective is to make sure that the test script follows exactly how the user interacts with the application. Utility methods start with an action, like sortAscending() and sortDescending(). Method names should not be plural unless the return type is a list or an array.

Variable Naming Conventions

Follow the camelCase rule. Name the variable exactly what it means. For example, if the variable is a list, name it as responseHeaders (note that name is plural). For single-value variables, you can use responseBody, responseContactType, responseStatusCode, jwtToken, and so on.

Constant Naming Conventions

Use all uppercase letters for constants. This indicates a differentiator from other variables.

Provide User Actions

Provide actual methods for actions, like login(); logout(), and authorize(); this will help in the readability of the test script.

Use getters and setters with the appropriate prefix: getResponse(); getJwtToken(); getJSON(); getTimeInMilliSeconds(); getCurrentDate(); setTestConfig(); and setJwtToken();.

Simplicity

Do not complicate a class or a method. It is good to have a single responsibility class or method. You can write many more methods that return only one thing. Organize them in such a way that refactoring will be easy.

Indentation

Indentation improves code readability. Use autoformatting of the code after the build, or before pushing it to the code repository. Use the following Maven plugin:

```
<plugin>
  <groupId>com.coveo</groupId>
  <artifactId>fmt-maven-plugin</artifactId>
  <version>2.5.1</version>
  <executions>
    <execution>
     <goals>
          <goal>format</goal>
     </goals>
    </execution>
  </executions>
</plugin>
```

In addition to above, I have a few more guidelines for test assertions and naming conventions for test scripts. Let's discuss them in the following sections.

Test Assertions

The best place for assertions is at the end of the test script.

Do not have any assertion helper methods in the test framework/ helper classes/utilities. Let the third-party assertion libraries (assertj) or the unit testing framework (JUnit, TestNG, etc.) do their work.

Test Class Naming Conventions

Prefix each test class based on the use case. For example, if you are testing CRUD operations, name them per the conventions in Table 8-1.

Table 8-1. *Test Class Naming Conventions*

Bad	Good	Comments
ContactTests, ContactOperationsTest, ContactCreateRead UpdateDeleteTest	CreateContactTest, ReadContactTest, UpdateContactTest, DeleteContactTest	The test name should be based on the user actions and should not be long, should not be technical, and should not sound like a unit test. It's better to have a single responsibility test class rather than doing multiple tests in a single class.

It is best to define rules and discuss them with the team/architect so that a better foundation can be laid out for upcoming or ongoing testing projects.

Test Method Naming Conventions

Prefix each test method based on the test summary of the test. For example, if you are testing create contact, it's best to name as per Table 8-2.

Table 8-2. Test Method Naming Conventions

Bad	Good	Comments
testResponesOfCreate Contact();	testAddContact();	The test name should be based on the user actions and should not be long, should not be technical, and should not sound like a unit test.
testAddAndUpdate Contact();	testAddContact();	Test one use case at a time.
test_add_contact();	testAddContact();	Do not use underscores; go with camelCase or per the coding guidelines of your team/organization.
testNullValuesCreate Contact();	testAddContactFirst NameNullValue();	Suffix the test with the actual value; this will help in directly understanding the issue if the test fails. Also, make sure that you are handling the exception properly.
testInvalidHeader CreateContact();	testAddContact InvalidAuthToken();	Naming the test method as per the test summary will help find the test/requirement failure easily without any effort.

Test method naming conventions are very important since you are working in scrum; you need to find the bugs as early as possible. It is very important that the failures should be interpreted quickly rather than making a guess about what is failing in the test script.

Test Package Naming Conventions

Maven projects, or any other project, must have a package structure or a folder structure; the package or folder name ends with `tests` or `tests.impl` (if you are implementing a base test or main test). It's best to name them as per Table 8-3.

Table 8-3. *Test Package Naming Conventions*

Bad	Good	Comments
com.contact.mgmt. tests.crud.tests	com.contact.mgmt. api.tests	Do not repeat the text "tests" in the package name twice; it should be the end of the tree.
com.contact.mgmt. tests.crud	com.contact.mgmt. api.tests	Always have the text "tests" as the last text in the package name unless you are implementing a base class.
com.contact.mgmt. crud_tests	com.contact.mgmt. api.tests	Do not use underscores in the package name.
com.contact.mgmt. crud-tests	com.contact.mgmt. api.tests	Do not use hyphens in the package name.
com.contact.mgmt. crud..impl.tests	com.contact.mgmt. api.tests.impl	If tests are implementing base or main test.

It is also good to use `api.tests` or `api.tests.impl` as the suffix with each test package. The package name should be all small characters and it should be singular if the contents are heterogeneous and plural if the contents are homogeneous.

We have discussed quite a bit on coding best practices and guidelines, but do you communicate this information with the team? This is where documentation is important. Maintain excellent documentation, which is required by the team for quality deliverables.

Documentation

Once framework development is done and a sample test script is working as expected, the next step is to document how to extend the framework with a new class/method/variable/constant/property/test data/etc. and how to add a new test script. Document all best practices, including everything discussed in the above sections. This will be helpful for any new team member. This will also be useful as a guide at a later time.

Documentation tools such as Google Docs, Confluence, or a wiki can be used. You can also use a GitHub repository, using markdown.

The document review should be done by the QA lead or the QA Architect.

Summary

In this chapter, you went through coding best practices as well as guidelines and test script naming conventions to follow while writing test scripts. You learned that for effective communication, documentation is a good way to keep everyone updated on how things need to be done. This also avoids ambiguities during discussions or team meetings. In the next chapter, you will start with test framework development from scratch.

CHAPTER 9

Organize a Test Framework

In the previous few chapters, you learned about several concepts of API testing including coding best practices, a good test script, and what needs to be tested in the API. In this chapter, you will learn about components of the test automation framework and its design aspects.

By the end of this chapter, you will know what an API test framework should contain and you will be able to write a test framework from scratch.

Frameworks enable a software engineer to write code with fewer lines faster and with ease. They improve the quality of the source code and software and they enhance productivity. With a good framework, boilerplate code can be reduced. A good framework helps in writing clean code.

Note Automation developers spend a lot of time developing test scripts. If the development takes a lot of time, you need to fix the test framework.

With a test framework, your objective is to write clean test scripts that are easier to read and are maintainable. A test script should be short and should follow the guidelines mentioned under section "Components of Test Script" in Chapter 7. A test framework is usable across other teams and is extensible for new requirements.

You will develop the test framework for the contact management application. Refer to Appendix B for instructions on deploying the application.

Let's work on the framework requirements in the following section.

Framework Requirements

The framework should allow you to send the request to the server with the required authentication and be able to read the response for doing assertions. It also allows different test configuration setups. If any error occurs, it should have the ability to throw a user-friendly exception. The framework should also support logging. Non-mandatory requirements include supporting static code analysis tools such as sonar.

Figure 9-1 shows the components of a typical test framework for API testing. The components are on the left side and the corresponding specifications are on the right side.

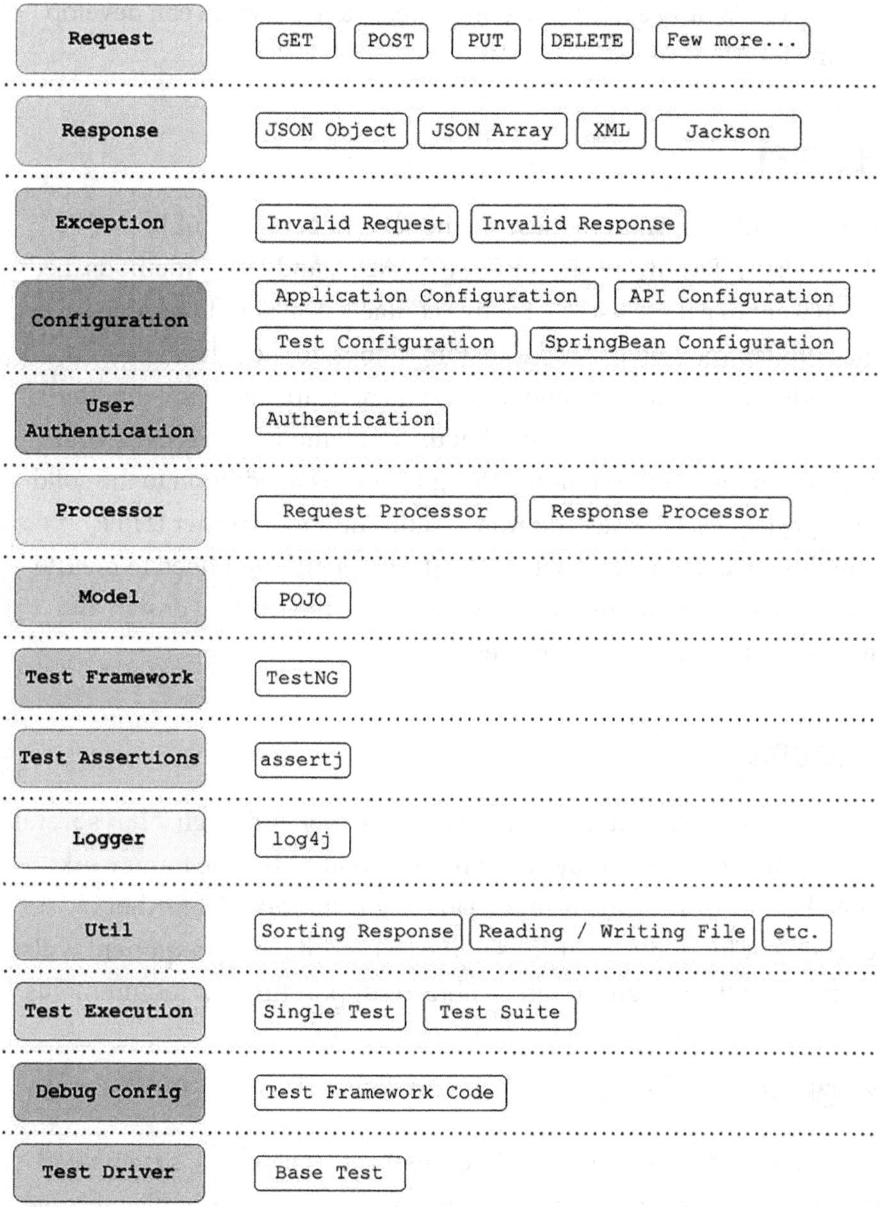

Request	GET	POST	PUT	DELETE	Few more...

Response	JSON Object	JSON Array	XML	Jackson

Exception	Invalid Request	Invalid Response

Configuration	Application Configuration	API Configuration
	Test Configuration	SpringBean Configuration

User Authentication	Authentication

Processor	Request Processor	Response Processor

Model	POJO

Test Framework	TestNG

Test Assertions	assertj

Logger	log4j

Util	Sorting Response	Reading / Writing File	etc.

Test Execution	Single Test	Test Suite

Debug Config	Test Framework Code

Test Driver	Base Test

Figure 9-1. *Components of a test framework*

117

Let's understand each of the components and how you can develop the same for API testing.

Request

A request is used to send requests to the server over HTTP `GET`, `POST`, `PUT`, `DELETE`, `PATCH`, `HEAD`, `OPTION CONNECT`, and `TRACE` methods. Let's say you want to get the list of all active contacts. You should be able to utilize this component to send a custom request to the server.

This is an important component so you need to make sure that the design is easy and extensible and that the implementation is clean and easy. You can utilize the standard design patterns in addition to the solid design principles. Let's say you want to add support for other HTTP methods with custom arguments. The developer doesn't need to rewrite the whole component; instead, they can utilize the existing design and extend the support for new requirements.

Response

This is the response sent to the client by the server. Although it has several formats, the most commonly used are JSON and XML. The framework should be able to store the response in the given format for further processing or for doing assertions in the test script. This component is also important, so the design should be able to support the new requirements.

Exception

The request and response at runtime can throw exceptions, so you need a custom exception handling technique that gives you a friendly message as and when an exception occurs. You just need two exception categories, like Request Exception and Response Exception, to make it easy while debugging.

Configuration

The test framework requires a test configuration, application endpoint, and more. This is supported by the Spring configuration and, like the above components, if you want to add a new configuration, it will be easier to just add a new class and have an instance in the Base Test.

User Authentication

Usually, user authentication is an implicit part of the request component. However, you need to make it clear and visible so that if any modifications are required at a later point of time, they can be done without impacting or touching any other component. If you want to test with different authentication types, it will be easier to add the required support.

Processor

You need a processor to process the given request and response in a way that is easy to comprehend. The processor is a very important component since this is the code that is exposed to the test scripts. You need to write the processor classes in a way that is like fluent API while writing the test script.

For example, you may want to do it all in a single line for a given request, as in the following line of code:

```
request().get(getUpdateContact(), 1001);
```

This is a request to the server over the HTTP GET method. The endpoint is /contact/{contactId}.

For a request, you may do it like this:

```
response().getResponse().getStatusCode();
```

This is a response from the server, and you are reading the status code returned to the client.

Model

With the help of the Jackson API, JSON-to-Java object mapping is easy, so you need a model class that can store the response JSON in a Java object.

The JSON response can be easily transformed into Java POJO using `https://freecodegenerators.com/code-converters/json-to-pojo`. Just paste the response in the JSON and click the Generate button; it will give you the required Java POJO. Add the empty and fully parameterized constructor and added your getter and setters. If the JSON has a child object or array, it will show you a new class. Do the same for each of the classes.

Note that there is no preference of converter. It's your choice. Just make sure to add the required constructor and getters/setters.

Test Framework

You need a XUnit test framework that supports test script development similar to the good test script we discussed in Chapter 7 under the section "Components of a Test Script." It should have `setup()`, `test()` and `tearDown()`. The test framework should also support running tests in parallel, whenever required.

Test Assertions

You need a test assertion framework that has good support for collections or data structures and does assertions fluently. Assertj is a test assertion API that has a good support.

For example, you may want to do the assertion for the response code given in the following line of code:

```
assertThat(response().getResponse().getStatusCode()).
isEqualTo(200);
```

Logger

It is good to have logger support, but it's not a mandatory requirement for writing test scripts. Log4j is extensively used in Java projects for logging purposes and is particularly useful while debugging.

Util

There will be requirements for the test script to generate time in milliseconds/seconds/minutes/hours/etc., or you may want to sort the response or do something else that is a routine requirement of the application testing. All of this can be a part of the test framework utility component.

Test Execution

You may need to execute a test individually, and more often than not as a suite, or you may want to just execute different test methods inside a test class. Ideally, all of them are provided implicitly by the test framework. If not, then you need to provide support for the same.

Debug Config

Maven has support for setting up a debug configuration. If you are using a programming language other than Java, you need support that can be enabled as and when required.

This is not a mandatory requirement, but it's good to have. If you use some of the standard packaging tools, this support comes implicitly.

Test Driver

You need a Base Test class that holds common code utilized by each of the test scripts. The base test does all the heavy lifting for the test script, which helps in writing a clean and clear test script with fewer lines of code. The entire test script can extend the base test and does the job of testing the use case efficiently.

You have now gone through all the components of an API test framework. Let's do the implementation in the following sections. You will start with the packaging and code management tool Maven.

Setting Up a Maven Project

You need a Maven project for managing test projects and building, installing, and executing test scripts/suites. Install Maven as per Appendix A.

Create a workspace directory called learn-api-test under your home directory and execute the following command in the terminal window:

```
$ mvn archetype:generate -DgroupId=com.learn.api.testing
-DartifactId=api-test -DarchetypeArtifactId=maven-archetype-
quickstart -DarchetypeVersion=1.4 -DinteractiveMode=false
```

This command will create a project named api-test under the current directory.

Let's add dependencies in the following section. This will be helpful in developing the components of the test framework.

Dependencies and Plugins

You are using RestAssured for API requests, the RestAssured Response for doing assertions, and Log4j for logging-related requirements. TestNG is the test framework that gives support for test suite/parallel test execution etc.; Java Spring Config for test and application configuration for reading the test properties and setting up the test environment; config. Assertj as the fluent assertion API; and Jackson as the response object storage. You will use these objects for storing the response and retrieving it during test assertions. The Maven compiler plugin compiles the code in the specific Java version. The Maven Surefire plugin is for test execution and debugging. An optional plugin is for code formatting.

Once the Maven project is created, add the dependencies under pom.xml as mentioned in the following sections.

RestAssured

You will use RestAssured to test API endpoints. Use version 4.5.0.

```
<dependency>
    <groupId>io.rest-assured</groupId>
    <artifactId>rest-assured</artifactId>
    <version>4.5.0</version>
</dependency>
```

Log4j

For logging messages, use Log4j. Use version 2.17.1 and above. Check the security vulnerability[1].

```
<dependency>
```

---

[1] https://logging.apache.org/log4j/2.x/security.html

```
        <groupId>org.apache.logging.log4j</groupId>
        <artifactId>log4j-api</artifactId>
        <version>2.17.1</version>
</dependency>
<dependency>
        <groupId>org.apache.logging.log4j</groupId>
        <artifactId>log4j-core</artifactId>
        <version>2.17.1</version>
</dependency>
```

TestNG

To write test scripts, use TestNG version 7.5.

```
<dependency>
        <groupId>org.testng</groupId>
        <artifactId>testng</artifactId>
        <version>7.5</version>
        <scope>test</scope>
</dependency>
```

Spring Framework

To test the configuration, use Spring Framework version 5.3.15.

```
<dependency>
        <groupId>org.springframework</groupId>
        <artifactId>spring-context</artifactId>
        <version>5.3.15</version>
</dependency>
<dependency>
        <groupId>org.springframework</groupId>
```

```
    <artifactId>spring-beans</artifactId>
    <version>5.3.15</version>
</dependency>
```

Assertj

For test assertions, use Assertj 3.9.1.

```
<dependency>
    <groupId>org.assertj</groupId>
    <artifactId>assertj-core</artifactId>
    <version>3.22.0</version>
    <scope>test</scope>
</dependency>
```

Jackson-Databind

To read the output from the response and store it in Java Bean, use Jackson-Databind for assertions. Use version 2.13.1.

```
<dependency>
    <groupId>com.fasterxml.jackson.core</groupId>
    <artifactId>jackson-databind</artifactId>
    <version>${jackson.version}</version>
</dependency>
```

Maven Compiler Plugin

Use the Maven compiler plugin to compile the source code of the Maven project. Specify the source and target the Java version based on your project requirements.

```
<plugin>
    <artifactId>maven-compiler-plugin</artifactId>
```

```
<version>3.9.0</version>
<configuration>
        <source>1.8</source>
        <target>1.8</target>
</configuration>
</plugin>
```

Surefire Plugin

Use the Surefire plugin to execute the tests. You can specify the directory where the report will be stored and the print summary Boolean flag. Setting it to true will print the summary of the test execution in the console.

```
<plugin>
    <groupId>org.apache.maven.plugins</groupId>
    <artifactId>maven-surefire-plugin</artifactId>
    <version>2.22.0</version>
    <configuration>
            <printSummary>true</printSummary>
            <reportsDirectory>test-output</reportsDirectory>
            <debugForkedProcess>true</debugForkedProcess>
    </configuration>
</plugin>
```

The print summary, if set to true, will show a summary of test execution results on the console. It's shown here:

```
Tests run: 1, Failures: 0, Errors: 0, Skipped: 0, Time elapsed:
2.638 s - in com.contact.mgmt.user.GetCurrentUserTest
```

The test execution report will be stored in the /test-output folder.

For debugging, you can enable the debugForkedProcess[2]. It will listen on port 5005 and you can start the debugger in Intellij using a debug pointer.

Java Code Formatting Plugin

The fmt-maven-plugin plugin does the formatting when you execute the test. Do not use it if you have an internal formatting or linting tool.

```
<plugin>
    <groupId>com.coveo</groupId>
    <artifactId>fmt-maven-plugin</artifactId>
    <version>2.13</version>
    <executions>
        <execution>
                <goals>
                        <goal>format</goal>
                </goals>
        </execution>
    </executions>
</plugin>
```

Take a look at the complete pom.xml located at https://github.com/Apress/Learn-API-Testing.

---

[2]https://maven.apache.org/surefire/maven-surefire-plugin/test-mojo.html#debugForkedProcess

Request

You need to develop code that can take the request parameters and provide the RestAssured response object. The request package has a scope for future extension, so you need to design this in a way that helps extensibility and follows design principles.

Common properties in all the request methods is that they will return the RestAssured response object. So, you can abstract this and put it in an interface or an abstract class and use the Factory design pattern[3] to your advantage for easy object creation. This also helps in extensibility. If you want to add a new type of request, you can add the implementation class and the rest will be the same.

Each request has a URL and a token; a few have additional parameters like query string or payload. This can be abstracted in an abstract class.

Now, you need to write the implementation class. Since you are using RestAssured, this class will have RestAssured API code that returns the RestAssured response object.

The input may be invalid for negative tests. Then, the implementation class will throw exceptions, such as a `JSONException` for an invalid payload and `IllegalArgumentException` for invalid query arguments. So, you need to add the exception in the abstract class or the interface you implemented.

You went through the RestAssured test script in Chapter 4. In the implementation class, you use the same code. The only thing that changes is that now it will be called by the test script rather than executed directly as a test script.

Let's take a quick look at the sample code snippets.

Request abstraction is done using an abstract class, which has the code shown here:

---

[3] https://en.wikipedia.org/wiki/Factory_method_pattern

```java
public abstract class HttpRequest {
 private String url;
 private String token;
 private Map<String, ? extends Object> query;
 private File payload;

 // getters and setters

 public abstract Response request() throws
 InvalidRequestException;
}
```

Next, you need to add the implementation class. Look at the code snippet below. You use the RestAssured API.

```java
public class GetRequestImpl extends HttpRequest {
 @Override
 public Response request() {
   Response response;
   try {
     response =
         given()
             .header("Authorization", "Bearer " + getToken())
             .contentType("application/json")
             .when()
             .get(getUrl());
   } catch (JSONException | IllegalArgumentException e) {
     log.error("error occurred while requesting " + getUrl());
     throw new InvalidRequestException("there is some problem
     with the request.", e);
   }
   return response;
 }
}
```

This implementation class implements the abstract method and this will be used in the test script to trigger the request. It throws the InvalidRequestException.

Next, you need to create a Factory class, which will provide the request object. Here is the sample code snippet:

```
public class HttpMethodFactory {
 public HttpRequest build(HttpMethodType type) {
   return type.createHttpRequest();
 }
}
```

It uses Java enums to create the required object based on the request. The following is the sample code snippet of the enum:

```
public enum HttpMethodType {
 GET {
   @Override
   public HttpRequest createHttpRequest() {
     return new GetRequestImpl();
   }
 },
 // few more here
 };

 public abstract HttpRequest createHttpRequest();
}
```

This code creates the instance of the implementation class based on the input.

You're using the Factory design pattern and confining the request object creation using the Factory class. The overall idea here is that you need to write request component code that is easy to understand, is extensible, and follows good design principles.

The last part is how the Base Test processes the request objects. For this, you need to create a request processor class. Take a look at the following code snippet:

```
public class RequestProcessor {
  private String jwtToken;
  private Response response;

  // getter and setter

  public void get(String endpoint) {
    HttpRequest httpGet = new HttpMethodFactory().
    build(HttpMethodType.GET);
    this.response = httpGet.setToken(jwtToken).setUrl(endpoint).
    request();
  }
}
```

This class provides the usage pattern for the test class.

The request should be packaged together in a meaningful way so that anyone who uses the API framework should be able to locate the required things easily.

Take a look at the complete source code for the request package in the GitHub project at https://github.com/Apress/Learn-API-Testing.

Response

RestAssured requests return the Response object. Response objects can be a JSON object or an array. So, you need a way to store and read the response for assertions.

Since you are using Jackson as the bean for storing and reading the response, the code should be extensible for future requirements. For example, if you find a new library or API that is better, then without major changes in the source code, you should be able to add support for the new library or the API.

You need to create an interface for each of the Java POJO object types and have an implementation class that does the actual work. This way, if in the future a new library or API is found to be useful, you can just quickly add support for it without changing any of the existing code base.

The contact management application response has a contact model, which is processed by Jackson-Databind. Each of these types returns different object types. The contact model will return a `Contact` and a `List<Contact>`.

You need to develop an abstract class for each of the response types, and you need a Response object getter and setter to get/set the response to and from the test script. If you look at the response types, you have two different types of responses. So, there will be two abstract classes and each abstract class will have an implementation class. This is a good example of a Factory design pattern that you implemented in the request package. But, now you need to get the object from the single source, so this is the best case for utilizing the Abstract Factory design pattern[4].

You need to create a few additional classes here: an `AbstractFactory` class and a `FactoryCreator` class. To fulfill the design principles, each of the abstract classes has to implement the request type interface, which we call as ResponseMarket.

Let's check out a code snippet of each of these classes.

The following is the abstract class:

```
public abstract class ContactResponse implements
ResponseMarker {
```

---

[4]https://en.wikipedia.org/wiki/Abstract_factory_pattern

```
private Response response;
// getter and setter

public abstract Contact getContact() throws
InvalidResponseException;
}
```

The Implementation class has the Jackson-Databind code and throws the InvalidResponseException:

```
public class ContactResponseImpl extends ContactResponse {
  @Override
  public Contact getContact() {
    ObjectMapper objectMapper = new ObjectMapper();
    Contact contact;
    try {
      contact = objectMapper.readValue(getResponse().asString(),
      Contact.class);
    } catch (JsonProcessingException e) {
      log.error("error occurred while reading the response
      array.");
      throw new InvalidResponseException("there is some problem
      with the response.", e);
    }
    return contact;
  }
}
```

The Factory class code is almost similar to the request factory classes. The only difference is you are creating a factory from the abstract factory, so you need an additional class named FactoryCreator. See the following code:

```
public class ResponseFactoryCreator {
```

```
private ResponseFactoryCreator() {}

public static ResponseAbstractFactory getFactory() {
  return new ResponseFactory();
 }
}
```

The last thing is the response processor, which is used by the test script. The response processor does the processing of the response sent from the server in a response object. Take a look at the following code snippet to see how the response is processed:

```
public class ResponseProcessor {
 ResponseAbstractFactory responseFactory =
ResponseFactoryCreator.getFactory();
 private Response response;

 // getter and setter

 public Contact getResponseContact() {
   return responseFactory.getContactResponse().
   setResponse(this.response).getContact();
 }
 // few more here
}
```

The highlighted line shows the usage of the response factory created through the response factory creator class.

As stated in the above section, the overall idea here is that you need to write response component code that is easy to understand, is extensible, and follows good design principles. Needless to say, it helps in building modular and reusable code.

Take a look at the complete source code for the response package in the GitHub project at https://github.com/Apress/Learn-API-Testing.

Exceptions

Request and response components will throw exceptions when you pass invalid request parameters or something bad happens. So, you need to add user-friendly exceptions which, when thrown, have a friendly message that helps in understanding what precisely went wrong.

You need to create InvalidRequestException and InvalidResponseException class files, which extend the RuntimeException standard exception class. Let's look at the code snippet of these classes:

```
public class InvalidRequestException extends RuntimeException {
 public InvalidRequestException(String errorMessage,
 Throwable err) {
   super(errorMessage, err);
 }
}

public class InvalidResponseException extends
RuntimeException {
 public InvalidResponseException(String errorMessage,
 Throwable err) {
   super(errorMessage, err);
 }
}
```

It is preferred to have custom exceptions for better readability of the code, and most importantly, it helps in debugging.

Configuration

You need to set the configuration of the project. This helps in testing multiple environments on the same endpoints with different or the same dataset. Configuration classes usually reside under src/test/java.

Let's go through the required configuration classes in the following section.

Properties File

Create an environment-specific properties file under src/test/resources under a directory named properties. Properties files will be specific to each of the environments. For example, dev.properties is for the development environment, test.properties is for the test environment, stage.properties is for the staging environment, and prod.properties is for the production environment. These property files have the test data for different environments.

Add another file named REST-endpoints.properties. This will store contact management application endpoints.

Add the following test property in the <env>.properties file. For now, you will be using only one URL for all environments. But in the real world, you will have different environments and different URLs, so the url property will change accordingly.

```
# URL
url=http://localhost:8080/app
```

Add the following properties in the REST-endpoints.properties file; these are the endpoints of the contact management sample web application:

```
# REST Endpoints
# Authentication
```

```
login=POST,/auth/authenticate
# Add Contact
contact.add=POST,/api/v1/contacts
# Contact List
contact.list=GET,/api/v1/contacts
# Find Contact
contact.find=GET,/api/v1/contacts/{id}
# Update Contact
contact.update=PUT,/api/v1/contacts/{id}
# Delete Contact
contact.delete=DELETE,/api/v1/contacts/{id}
```

Take a look at the configuration properties located at https://github.
com/Apress/Learn-API-Testing.

Let's discuss the config classes in the following sections.

Spring

The Java Spring configuration is used for loading the properties file. It
helps in setting up environment-specific test data while running tests.

For example, if you want to run smoke tests on specific environments
from the command prompt, you can pass a value to the given variable,
Denv=<environment>, and the test data present in <environment>.
properties file will be loaded for test execution.

Create a package in src/test/java named com.contact.mgmt.api.
config and create a Java file named SpringBeanConfiguration. Add the
following lines of code:

```
@Configuration
@ComponentScan
public class SpringBeanConfiguration {

  @Bean
```

```
 public static PropertySourcesPlaceholderConfigurer
propertyConfig() {
   return new PropertySourcesPlaceholderConfigurer();
 }
}
```

This is the standard code provided by org.springframework for a properties file configuration.

Next, you need to create a config class that will use the properties file at runtime. Create another Java file named TestConfig in the same package and add the following lines of code:

```
@Configuration
@PropertySource("classpath:properties/${env}.properties")
public class TestConfig {

 @Value("${url}")
 private String url;

 public String getUrl() {
    return url;
 }
}
```

Check the annotation @PropertySource. It has a path to the properties file, which will be used to set environment-specific test data.

The value of the environment variable ${env} will be picked up from the command prompt with values viz., dev, test, stage, and prod, respectively.

Check the following example. In this command, the environment is set to test. This is the test environment on which the tests will get executed.

```
-Denv=test
```

Application Configuration

You need to access the contact management endpoints, and for that you need to create another configuration file. Name it ContactManagementConfig.java and create a Java class in the package com.contact.mgmt.api.config. This class will be used for reading the API endpoints. Here is the sample code snippet from the ContactManagementConfig class:

```
@Configuration
@PropertySource("classpath:properties/REST-endpoints.
properties")
public class ContactManagement {
  @Value("${login}")
  private String LOGIN;

  @Value("${contact.add}")
  private String ADD_CONTACT;

  public String authentication() {
    return LOGIN.split(",")[1];
  }

  public String addContact() {
    return ADD_CONTACT.split(",")[1];
  }
}
```

The first line reads the endpoints properties file; this is the standard way of reading the properties file in spring config.

The second line reads the property login from the rest API endpoints properties file and stores it into the local variable LOGIN.

Authentication is done by the following lines of code:

```
public String authentication() {
    return LOGIN.split(",")[1];
}
```

It returns the login auth/authenticate endpoint to the caller. You call split because you need to read the string after the comma, which is the actual endpoint. Look at the REST-endpoints.properties in the following section for the properties.

Application Context

You need to set the Spring application context. ApplicationContext.java does the required job for you. It gives you access to the TestConfig and ContactManagement objects, which are called from the test script. Add this class under the same package as the other config files, com.contact.mgmt. api.config.

Application Config

The application config will help in providing the complete URL of the application with the help of ApplicationContext, which returns the URL, and ContactManagementConfig, which returns the endpoint. Check the following code snippet of AppConfig.java. This class also needs to be added in the com.contact.mgmt.api.config package.

```
public class AppConfig {
 private static ApplicationContext applicationContext = new
ApplicationContext();

 public static String getUrl() {
    return applicationContext.getUrl();
 }
```

```
public static ContactManagementConfig
getContactManagementConfig() {
   return applicationContext.getContactManagementConfig();
 }
}
```

Complete URL For the Test Script

Now you need to get the complete URL of the endpoint in the test script. This can be done by an enum class, as shown in following code snippet of ContactManagement.java. Add this class under the same package as the other config classes you added in prior sections. You will see the usage of this class in the next chapter when you write the first test script.

```
public enum ContactManagement {
 ADD_CONTACT {
   @Override
   public String url() {
     return AppConfig.getUrl() + AppConfig.
     getContactManagementConfig().addContact();
   }
 },
 UPDATE_CONTACT {
   @Override
   public String url() {
     return AppConfig.getUrl() + AppConfig.
     getContactManagementConfig().updateContact();
   }
 },
 FIND_CONTACT {
   @Override
   public String url() {
```

```
    return AppConfig.getUrl() + AppConfig.
    getContactManagementConfig().findContact();
  }
},
GET_ACTIVE_CONTACTS {
  @Override
  public String url() {
    return AppConfig.getUrl() + AppConfig.
    getContactManagementConfig().getActiveContacts();
  }
},
DELETE_CONTACT {
  @Override
  public String url() {
    return AppConfig.getUrl() + AppConfig.
    getContactManagementConfig().deleteContact();
  }
};

public abstract String url();
}
```

Take a look at the complete source code of config classes located at https://github.com/Apress/Learn-API-Testing.

Test Data

You need test data to test the application. For example, for login and to get the token, you need to have an authentication payload. To create or update a contact, you need a request payload.

The next sections show examples for storing the test data.

JSON File

Add a folder under src/test/resources as authentication, create a JSON file named adminPayload.json, and add the following contents to the JSON file:

```
{
  "userName": "admin",
  "password": "test123"
}
```

This is the userName and password payload for auth/authenticate on the auth server. This is the only user you have in the contact management application.

auth/authenticate will send the JWT after a successful login.

Payload for POST and PUT HTTP Methods

Add a folder under src/test/resources named payload/contact, create JSON files named contact.json and updateContact.json, and add the following contents to the JSON file. You will use these JSON files in the test script as a payload for the POST and PUT requests.

contact.json
```
{
  "firstName": "Jagdeep",
  "lastName": "Jain",
  "email": "jj@gmail.com"
}
```

update_contact.json
```
{
  "firstName": "Praveen",
  "lastName": "Jain",
  "email": "pj@gmail.com"
}
```

Take a look at the complete source code in the GitHub project at https://github.com/Apress/Learn-API-Testing.

User Authentication

Authentication is the entry point in the test script. Each test script starts with setting up the user authentication and then hitting the endpoint. This class wraps the RestAssured API and provides the JWT token for accessing the endpoints. This will return the response RestAssured object, and from this object you can get the JWT token.

Create a class named Authentication under com.contact.mgmt. api.auth. The following is the RestAssured code showing how the authentication is done:

```
public Authentication init() {
 String endPoint = getTestConfig().getUrl() +
getContactManagement().authentication();
 try {
   String requestPayload = "src/test/resources/authentication/
   adminPayload.json";
   Response response =
       given()
           .body(new File(requestPayload))
           .contentType("application/json")
           .when()
           .post(endPoint);
   this.response = response;
   this.jwtToken = response.getHeader("Authorization");
   setJwtToken(this.jwtToken);
 } catch (JSONException | IllegalArgumentException e) {
   log.error("error occurred in authentication.");
```

```
throw new InvalidRequestException(
    "there is some problem with " + "the " +
    "authentication.", e);
}
return this;
}
```

You pass the JSON payload as a file and therefore the body has the
File object.

application/json is the content type of the payload.

url is the application URL under test.

Take a look at the authentication class in the GitHub project at
https://github.com/Apress/Learn-API-Testing.

Processor

This is the most important part of the test framework. It helps you to write
clean test scripts with minimal lines of code. You need a fluent way of
accessing the request and response. I discussed the request and response
processor in the above sections when discussing the request and response
classes.

The RequestProcessor class helps in requesting the resource from
the test script. It consists of HTTP methods, which are called from the
test script.

The ResponseProcessor class processes the responses for fluent
assertions. These classes act as a bridge between the RestAssured APIs, the
response processor implementation, and the test script.

You will explore the usage in the next chapter.

Model

Jackson-Databind does the JSON-to-Java object conversion, and for that you need to have the model class that can store the response as a Java object. So, you need to create a Contact model as a POJO (Plain Old Java Object[5]).

Take a look at the model package for Contact POJO. This will store the response processed by Jackson-Databind.

Test Framework

You expect the test framework to do all the routine work for you. TestNG is one of the popular test frameworks in the Java community. Let's understand what it needs for efficient test case development and execution.

You need to add a testing XML file to set up the test suite. This needs to be added for executing a test suite in the Maven profile.

Create a new file named `build-acceptance-tests.xml` under `src/test/resources/test-suite/` folder and add the following contents to the file. You will add the test name in the next chapter.

```
<?xml version="1.0" encoding="UTF-8"?>
<!DOCTYPE suite SYSTEM "http://testng.org/testng-1.0.dtd">
<suite name="Contact Management Build Acceptance Tests"
parallel="tests" thread-count="10">
  <test name="Auth API Tests">
    <classes>
      <class name=""/>
    </classes>
  </test>
</suite>
```

---

[5]https://en.wikipedia.org/wiki/Plain_old_Java_object

Add the following lines of code in pom.xml to test the test suite:

```
<profiles>
  <profile>
    <id>buildAcceptance</id>
    <build>
      <plugins>
        <plugin>
          <groupId>org.apache.maven.plugins</groupId>
          <artifactId>maven-surefire-plugin</artifactId>
         <version>${maven.surefire.plugin.version}</version>
          <configuration>
            <suiteXmlFiles>
            <suiteXmlFile>src/test/resources/test-suites/
            build-acceptance-tests.xml</suiteXmlFile>
            </suiteXmlFiles>
          </configuration>
        </plugin>
      </plugins>
    </build>
  </profile>
</profiles>
```

In the sections above, you added all the required components to the test framework.

You can download the complete source code from the GitHub repository at https://github.com/Apress/Learn-API-Testing.

Logger

Add the log4j.xml file under src/java/main/resources and the log4j-test.xml in src/test/java/resources and add the following lines of code. This is the logging configuration for logging on the console. The configuration is self-explanatory. For more information, follow the official document at https://logging.apache.org/log4j/2.x/manual/configuration.html.

```xml
<?xml version="1.0" encoding="UTF-8"?>
<Configuration xmlns="http://logging.apache.org/log4j/2.0/config">
  <Properties>
    <Property name="CONSOLE_LOG_PATTERN">
      %-5p | %d{yyyy-MM-dd HH:mm:ss} | [%t] %C{2}
      (%F:%L) - %m%n
    </Property>
  </Properties>
  <Appenders>
    <Console name="console" target="SYSTEM_OUT">
      <PatternLayout
            pattern="${CONSOLE_LOG_PATTERN}" />
    </Console>
  </Appenders>
  <Loggers>
    <Logger name="com.contact.mgmt" level="info" />
    <Logger name="org.springframework" level="error"/>
    <Root level="warn">
      <AppenderRef ref="console" />
    </Root>
  </Loggers>
</Configuration>
```

The important thing is to understand the logging level; you use the logging level as info for all the files under the com.contact.mgmt package and error for org.springframework.

Util

You need to have the utility class for routine work like sorting the response and such. This class can be added under src/main/java in the util package. Here is the sample code snippet of the Util class:

```
public class Util {
 private Util() {}
 public static List<String> sortList(List<String> list) {
   Collections.sort(list);
   return list;
 }
}
```

Making the functions as static gives the ability to call them without creating the instance of the class.

Test Execution

TestNG and Maven have excellent support for test execution. You can create a test suite in TestNG and supply this test suite as an XML file to the Maven profile. Maven has various options to execute the test suite and the test case. Even at the method level, you can execute a test provided that the test method has no dependency.

Debug Config

While working on adding dependencies and plugins under Maven Surefire headings, you learned that if you set the debugForkedProcess flag as true, you can debug the test execution path. You will explore debugging in the next chapter when you write the first test script.

Test Driver

A test driver is a concept that is used for driving the test scripts by providing all the helpful methods that are routine for a test script. You will be developing the BaseTest class in the next chapter, which has all the routines that are required by the test script. The BaseTest class is the driver of test scripts.

Summary

In this chapter, you went through the components of the test framework and how to organize it. You added required dependencies for assertions, testing, and all other required components that you need for writing a test script. You added all of the required components for testing API endpoints, such as requests, responses, HTTP authentication, and HTTP methods GET, POST, PUT, and DELETE. You also added support for reading the response and how the request and response are processed in the test script. With the help of the Spring Bean configuration, you learned that you can execute tests in different environments.

In the next chapter, you will write your first test script, execute it, and check the results.

CHAPTER 10

First Test Script

In the previous chapter, you developed a test framework from scratch. This chapter is an extension of that chapter. Now you will develop the first test script, execute it, and verify the results.

At the end of this chapter, you should have a good knowledge of how to write a test script that takes less development time, is easy to develop, and has all the characteristics of a good test script.

For a test framework to be successful, a tester should be able to write test scripts that are readable, require fewer lines of code, and take less development time.

As mentioned in the previous chapter, a test script should have the minimum lines of codes possible and follow the guidelines mentioned under the section "Components of Test Script" in Chapter 7.

The following sections offer the foundation for developing test scripts.

Developing Your First Test

A test script has the following steps for testing the endpoint:

1. Application URL.

2. Login user details.

3. Authentication.

4. JWT token.

© Jagdeep Jain 2022
J. Jain, *Learn API Testing*, https://doi.org/10.1007/978-1-4842-8142-0_10

5. Pass the JWT token as the request header in the request.

6. Request endpoint with required query, payload, and so on.

7. Read the response.

8. Do the assertions on the response object.

For test scripts, these steps should be seamless and should include local variables storing the application URL, user details, storing the JWT token, passing in the request, and so on. You already developed a mechanism for test config as config classes with the help of a Java Spring configuration. A request and response processor will do the job of processing the request and response. Assertions should be a part of the test script and cannot be common code.

All of these steps are required for each test scripts, so you can put the steps in a common class and then utilize the common code from the test scripts. Name the common class as BaseTest.java.

Let's work on the BaseTest.java class in the following section.

Base Test

In the previous chapter, you developed the framework from scratch. Now, let's extend it.

Add BaseTest.java under src/test/java in the package com.contact.mgmt.api.tests and add the code for authentication, request methods, and capturing the response. Each of the test scripts will extend the BaseTest class.

Authentication

Authentication is straightforward and requires a single line in the
BaseTest class:

```
protected void authentication() {
  this.jwtToken = new Authentication().init().getJwtToken();
}
```

The BaseTest class stores the JWT in the local variable for the request
processor.

Request Processor

The request processor should be fluent, which helps in writing fewer lines
of code. Initialize the request processor and add the following method:

```
private RequestProcessor requestProcessor;

protected RequestProcessor request() {
  requestProcessor = new RequestProcessor();
  requestProcessor.setJwtToken(this.jwtToken);
  return requestProcessor;
}
```

This method returns the request processor object and helps in the
fluent call to the request method.

Response Processor

Once the API has requested the resource from the server, you need to
have a way to store the server response. The request processor object has
the response object. You need to set the response object in the request
processor.

The following method does the job of processing the response for the test script:

```
protected ResponseProcessor response() {
  ResponseProcessor responseProcessor = new ResponseProcessor();
  this.response = requestProcessor.getResponse();
  responseProcessor.setResponse(this.response);
  return responseProcessor;
}
```

This method returns the response processor object and helps in a fluent call to the response methods.

Apart from this, you can add the getJwtToken(), set JwtToken(), getResponse(), and setResponse() methods. This will be useful in negative testing.

This is all you need for a test script. Take a look at the source code of auth, config, and BaseTest classes in the GitHub project at https://github.com/Apress/Learn-API-Testing.

First Test

Let's work on the create contact test case. The following are the steps for creating a contact using the API endpoint:

1. Log in using admin.

2. Get the JWT token.

3. Call HTTP POST to create contact API endpoint /api/v1/contacts with a payload

    ```
    {
      "firstName": "Jagdeep",
      "lastName": "Jain",
      "email": "jj@gmail.com"
    }
    ```

and pass JWT as the bearer in the
Authorization header.

4.   Verify the response status code as 201.

You need a valid JWT, the payload for a new contact, and the endpoint.
All are part of the BaseTest class.

Before starting the test script development, you need to add the
payload JSON under src/test/resources/, create a folder structure as
payload/contact/, and add the contact.json file, which has details of
the contact you want to add in the contact management application.

Create a new test class Java file called CreateContactTest.java,
extending the BaseTest class under the package com.contact.mgmt.
api.tests.

Recall from Chapter 7 that you need to add setup() and test().
For now, you don't need tearDown() since you are not resetting any
configuration. Since you are using JWT for authentication, the token will
be valid until the expiry of the timestamp. So, if you forcibly invalidate or
blacklist the token, the test scripts will start failing since the tests will be
running in parallel. You do not want to forcibly invalidate the token.

It is good to run the invalid JWT test after the test suite execution is
complete. Moreover, this may be a duplicate effort if security testing is also
testing the authentication as a part of the security test plan.

The following is the code snipped from the test script:

```
public class CreateContactTest extends BaseTest {

@BeforeTest
public void setup() {
    authentication();
}

@Test(description = "verify response of POST /api/v1/
contacts", priority = 1)
```

```
public void testAddContact() {
    String NEW_CONTACT = "src/test/resources/payload/contact" +
    "/contact" + ".json";
    request().post(ContactManagement.ADD_CONTACT.url(),
    new File(NEW_CONTACT));

    assertThat(response().getResponse().getStatusCode()).
    isEqualTo(201);
    assertThat(response().getResponse().getStatusLine()).
    isEqualTo("HTTP" + "/1.1 " + "201 ");
  }
}
```

Inside the setup() method, you are calling the authentication() method to get the JWT token. The BaseTest class will store the JWT token in the instance variable.

Inside the testAddContact() method, since you already have the JWT token in the context of the BaseTest class, you can now call the HTTP POST method on the contact management application to create a contact.

The HTTP request is shown by the highlighted code in the test method. You can see that it's a fluent call that increases the readability of the test script and improves the development time.

You also want everyone in the team to understand the test at the first glance, so you need to add the description.

The following line of code shows how you need to add a summary of the test in a single line. This should be part of the software test automation best practices.

```
@Test(description = "verify response of POST /api/v1/contacts",
priority = 1)
```

Look at the test script. It is just a single-line test. You just call the POST HTTP method and then perform the assertions. All the routine stuff is taken care of by the BaseTest class. This is how you need to write test scripts going forward for the remaining endpoints.

Take a look at the complete source code at GitHub location https://github.com/Apress/Learn-API-Testing.

You have developed the first test, and if you continue at this speed, in a couple of minutes, a number of tests will be ready; all of them belong to some test suite or the other.

Let's discuss developing a test suite in the following section.

Test Suite

TestNG has various options that help in configuring the test suite as per your needs. Let's explore how to do it.

TestNG XML

You need to create a TestNG XML file under the /resources/test-suite/ folder. Create a build-acceptance.xml file and add the following content:.

```
<?xml version="1.0" encoding="UTF-8"?>
<!DOCTYPE suite SYSTEM "http://testng.org/testng-1.0.dtd">
<suite name="Contact Management Dry Run Tests" parallel="tests"
       thread-count="1">
   <test name="Create Contact API Tests">
      <classes>
          <class name="com.contact.mgmt.api.tests.
          CreateContactTest"/>
      </classes>
   </test>
</suite>
```

TestNG helps in executing tests in parallel at the test, class, or method level. You can specify the level in the parallel parameter in the XML. You can also specify the thread count with the thread-count parameter.

You also need to specify the TestNG XML file path in the pom.xml inside the build tag. When a profile is included in the Maven command, it executes the test suite specified in the TestNG file.

The following is the code snippet of the Maven profile:

```
<profile>
    <id>e2e</id>
    <build>
        <plugins>
            <plugin>
                <groupId>org.apache.maven.plugins</groupId>
                <artifactId>maven-surefire-plugin</artifactId>
                <version>${maven.surefire.plugin.version}
                </version>
                <configuration>
                    <suiteXmlFiles>
                        <suiteXmlFile>
                            src/test/resources/test-suites/
                            build-acceptance.xml
                        </suiteXmlFile>
                    </suiteXmlFiles>
                </configuration>
            </plugin>
        </plugins>
    </build>
</profile>
```

Take a look at the complete pom.xml at GitHub location https:// github.com/Apress/Learn-API-Testing.

Executing a Test

Once you have developed the test scripts for a given feature under a test, you can create a test suite and execute all of the tests using a single command. The following section shows how to execute the test suite as well as an individual test script.

Execute a Test Suite

Execute the following command in the terminal window to execute the test suite:

```
$ mvn clean test -Pe2e -Denv=test
```

mvn clean test is the standard command to execute the test(s).

mvn -Pe2e is used to pass the Maven profile, which is configured with TestNG XML.

-Denv is used to pass the environment on which you need to execute the test script.

Execute an Individual Test

Execute the following command in the terminal window to run an individual test:

```
$ mvn clean test -Dtest=CreateContactTest -Denv=test
```

Since you are using Maven as a tool for building and packaging, you have all the Maven commands at your disposal.

-Dtest is used to pass the test class name.

For more commands, refer to the Maven documentation[1].

---

[1] https://maven.apache.org/guides/getting-started/maven-in-five-minutes.html#running-maven-tools

159

Execution Results

TestNG provides a good HTML report of execution results. Let's look at the TestNG execution report in the following section.

TestNG Report

In Chapter 9, you configured the TestNG report in the "Dependencies and Plugins" section under the /test-output folder. Open the index.html file and check the execution results, shown in Figure 10-1.

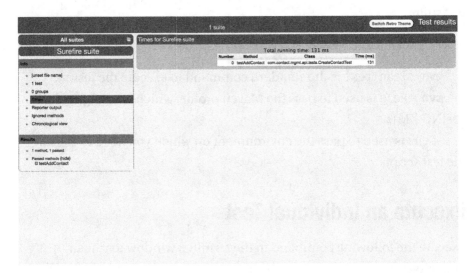

Figure 10-1. *Surefire test results*

Under the Results left-hand menu, you can see 1 method, 1 passed and you can see the name of the method as well.

Logging

While developing tests, invariably you want to check the request and response. RestAssured provides a method that can be used to check the execution logs:

log().all()

```
given().log().all()
    .header("Authorization", "Bearer " + auth)
    .contentType("application/json")
    .when()
    .get(url, param);
```

This code snippet shows how to use log().all() in the request code. Execution results are shown in the following console output:

```
[INFO] Running com.contact.mgmt.api.tests.CreateContactTest
Request method:    POST
Request URI:    http://localhost:8080/app/api/v1/contacts
Proxy:          <none>
Request params:    <none>
Query params:      <none>
Form params:       <none>
Path params:       <none>
Headers:        Authorization=Bearer eyJhbGciOiJIUzI1NiJ9.
eyJzdWIiOiJhZG1pbiIsImV4cCI6MTY0NTI2MTUwNCwiaWF0IjoxNjQ1Mj
U5NzAofQ.pHl3OBgOBejSv8sJ4LIKgdQFxnQacMyLKyoK96QuXcw
                            Accept=*/*
                            Content-Type=application/json
Cookies:                <none>
Multiparts:             <none>
```

Body:
src/test/resources/payload/contact/contact.json
[INFO] Tests run: 1, Failures: 0, Errors: 0, Skipped: 0,
Time elapsed: 4.128 s - in com.contact.mgmt.api.tests.
CreateContactTest

Response Time

RestAssured provides the time() and timeIn() methods that can be used to measure the response time. This can be used for assertions if you want to make sure that the response time is not exceeding the maximum response time.

Look at the following lines of code:

```
Response response =
    given()
        .body(payload)
        .header("Authorization", "Bearer " + auth)
        .contentType("application/json")
        .when()
        .post(url);

log.info(response.time());
log.info(response.timeIn(TimeUnit.SECONDS));
```

This will print the response time. TimeUnit has other options so you can get time in MILLISECONDS, MICROSECONDS, NANOSECONDS, DAYS, HOURS, and MINUTES.

Debug

Once in a while, when the individual test or the test suite fails, you need to debug the test script. The following steps help in setting up the debugger in the Intellij IDE:

1. Click Run ➤ Edit Configuration.

2. Click the plus icon (+) and select Remote JVM Debug.

3. Enter api-test-config as the name.

4. Update Host to localhost and Post as 5005 (if not set already).

5. Click Ok.

These steps create a debug configuration that is used during the debugging.

Open pom.xml and update <debugForkedProcess>true</debugForkedProcess> to true.

Now execute the test from the command prompt. It will show you the following in the terminal window:

```
-------------------------------------------------------
 T E S T S
-------------------------------------------------------
Listening for transport dt_socket at address: 5005
```

Once you get the message in the console that the test is listening on the port 5005, click the debugger icon in the IDE. If you have set up the debug pointer, the test will stop on the pointer and you have the option to resume or end the test.

In the IDE, it will look like Figure 10-2.

163

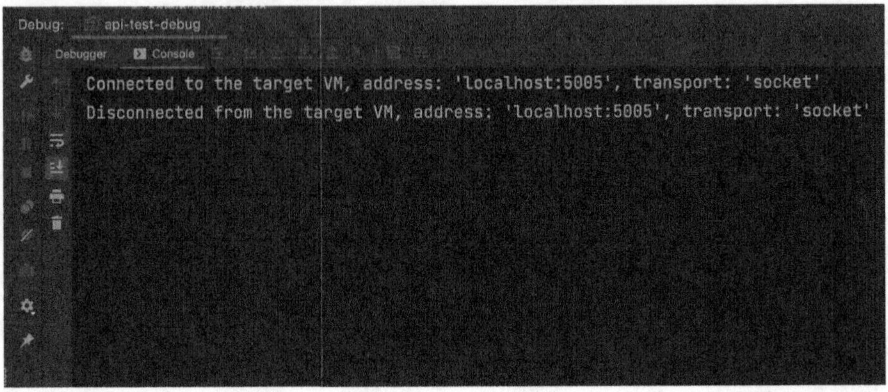

```
Debug:      api-test-debug

    Debugger    ▶ Console

         Connected to the target VM, address: 'localhost:5005', transport: 'socket'
         Disconnected from the target VM, address: 'localhost:5005', transport: 'socket'
```

Figure 10-2. *Intellij IDE console*

Summary

In this chapter, you learned how to extend the test framework and add a BaseTest class that does the work required for a test script. You also added TestNG XML to create a test suite. You learned how to run a single test as well as a test suite. You also saw where to look for execution reports. You now know about RestAssured's log().all() and response.time() methods and how to debug a test execution.

This chapter officially concludes learning API testing. In the next chapter, you will go through how to check and use API documentation for API testing.

CHAPTER 11

API Documentation

From Chapter 2 to Chapter 10, you learned about a web application, its architecture, authentication, requests, responses, practices, standards, and guidelines for effective test automation. You explored different tools like cURL, Postman, and RestAssured. You now understand the API testing paradigm (internal/external APIs, consumer-driven contract testing, etc.). With this, you learned how to perform API testing. However, you have not covered how the tester is informed about what to test in the API. If there is a change in the endpoint, payload, or model, how will the tester be informed of the new changes? In this chapter, you'll explore API documentation, which will be developed using the Swagger UI[1], and how to read the documentation, which will be useful when writing test scripts.

At the end of this chapter, you will have a solid understanding of how to read API documentation using Swagger, which is one of the most popular API documentation tools in the software industry.

It is a standard practice for any API development team to build documentation of the endpoints. It is particularly useful when the API endpoints are exposed to the external world.

API documentation should be one of the mandatory requirements for writing API tests. In the following sections, you will explore the need for API documentation and how to read the Swagger API documentation for better understanding and testing.

---

[1] `https://swagger.io/`

Need

In agile methodology, we define requirements as a user story. For example, say a user of an Amazon mobile app wants to add a product to their wish list. This single line story helps the development team to understand the requirement before providing working code.

Once the story development starts, numerous development artifacts are produced and they are compiled into a document describing the APIs. The document is shared and consumed among other teams. In the event an individual develops such a document on their own, they are likely to develop the document according to their own limited understanding and pass it on to the teams who are consuming the API endpoint(s). In the worst case scenario, there will be a great deal of back and forth on the clarity of the document. Moreover, if any definition changes but the individual developer forgets to update the change in the document, it will translate into a nightmare for the team consuming it. And this is so far just about the developer who is trying to access the API. When the document gets to the tester and the definition is again changed (in agile development, changes are inevitable), it will impact the release of the product and add to the cost of testing.

Another significant point is that each team may follow a different documentation style. So how to communicate effectively is another aspect that needs to be looked into.

You need a standard approach towards API documentation. A standard for API documentation will not only help the consuming development team but also the other stakeholders to correctly interpret the behavior of an API.

In the next section, you will explore the Swagger UI, which has great features for a development team and is highly configurable as well.

Swagger

The biggest advantage with Swagger is that it provides a way to self-describe the structure of the endpoint.

Refer to Appendix B to launch the contact management application, Swagger. It will look like Figure 11-1.

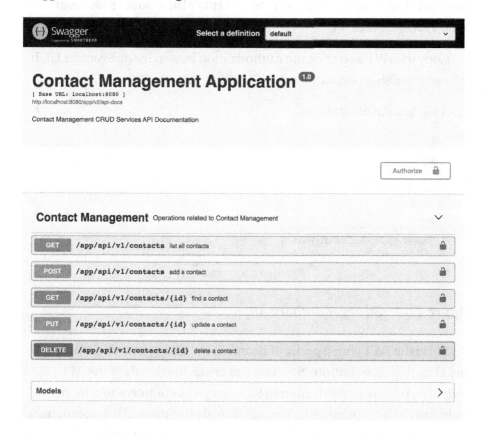

Figure 11-1. *Swagger's UI*

In Figure 11-1, the API documentation shows five endpoints. It also shows a visual and colorful representation of the API endpoints. It has the HTTP method, the endpoint URI, and a short description of what the API endpoint does.

Contact management endpoints are secure in Swagger. It requires a bearer token for authorization. Secured APIs can be accessed with the valid JWT only, and you can obtain the JWT from the cURL command.

Enter the following command in the terminal window:

```
$ curl -d '{"userName": "admin", "password": "test123"}' -H
'Content-Type: application/json' http://localhost:8080/app/
auth/authenticate -v
```

Copy the JWT and click the Authorization button in the Swagger UI. It will open a dialog box, as shown in Figure 11-2.

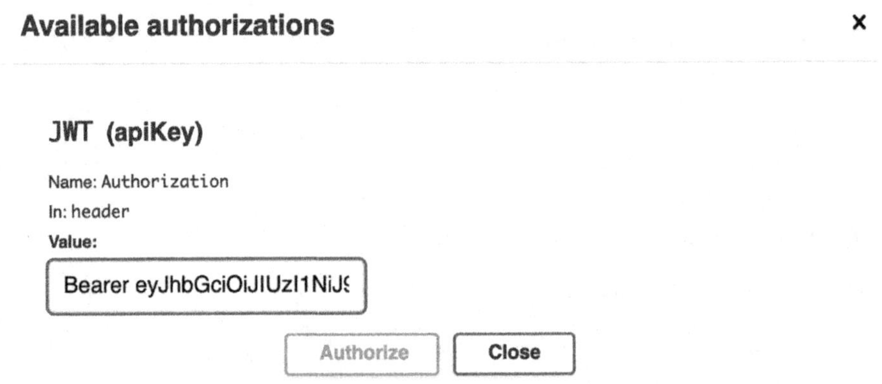

Available authorizations   ✕

JWT (apiKey)

Name: Authorization

In: header

Value:

Bearer eyJhbGciOiJIUzI1NiJ£

Authorize   **Close**

Figure 11-2. *Swagger authorization*

Enter the JWT with a prefix of Bearer in the dialog box, click Authorize, and click the Close button. Now you can check the details of the API endpoint. Having authorization in Swagger gives completeness to the endpoints' cURL commands. You can directly use these cURL commands given on the Swagger UI page and execute the same for testing.

Besides endpoints representation, it shows the entity or the model used in the application. The bottom of the page shows a contact model. See Figure 11-3. It has a contact model for a request and a response. Expanding the models shows the respective payload for the request and the response.

Figure 11-3. Swagger models

The Swagger UI is configurable and you can hide the details if you don't want to share them with other teams. Hide information that is not required for testing or not requested by other teams. Otherwise, this information will attract a lot of questions, and testing additional items will take a lot of time.

Let's get into the details of the first endpoint, which gets a list of all contacts. The endpoint is GET/api/v1/contacts. Click the endpoint.

Details of the endpoints are shown in Figure 11-4. You can see the response codes and the description having a valid model. This is where the tester has to note down what each response means associated with the response code. The tester has to derive the scenarios that represent these responses.

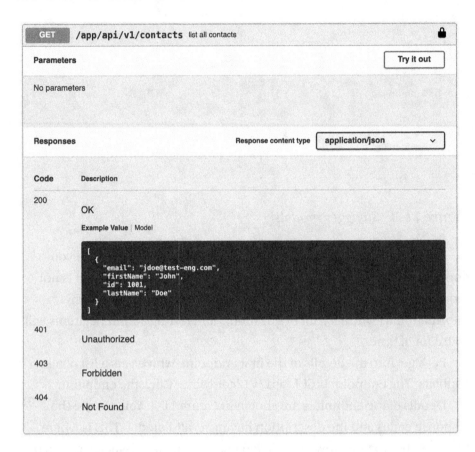

Figure 11-4. *GET request*

Swagger also gives you an option to try the API. Click the "Try it out" button and it will give you an option to execute the API. This is a really cool feature and can facilitate checking the results of the API implementation without much effort. In short, it gives you visibility into how the API behaves based on a given input.

Click the Execute button and you will see the screen shown in Figure 11-5.

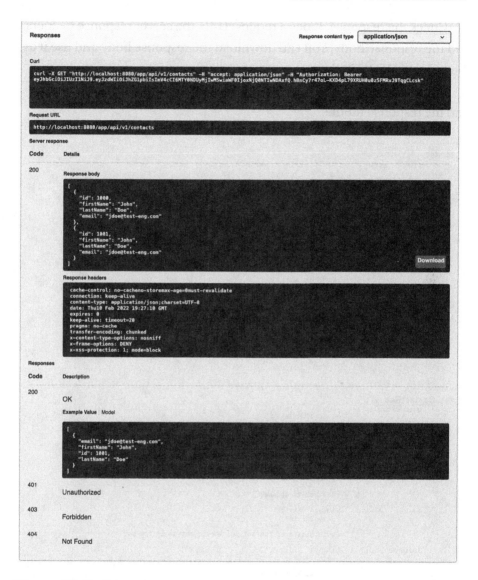

Figure 11-5. *Swagger response*

Figure 11-5 shows a complete cURL command, including the bearer token. You can use this command without any changes and it will work as expected.

Check the response. It has a request URL, the server response headers, and the response body. You can download the response body and use it as the expected JSON in the test script assertions.

Look at the model in Figure 11-6. It shows the contact request model and the response model.

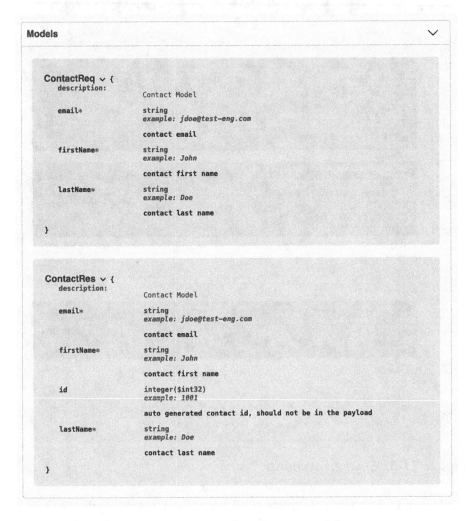

Figure 11-6. Swagger request and response models

When the contact is created, an autogenerated id is assigned by the back-end code and that's why it is not required, and therefore not shown, in the Swagger UI.

The contact response model has an id, which you retrieve when you do an HTTP GET to list all contacts.

The model also has information on the mandatory fields, which you can use to write the test plan for mandatory field tests. You can also check the data type of the parameters in the model. This information can be used for writing tests around data types.

Look at the HTTP PUT in Figure 11-7 for updating a contact. It has a parameter in the URL that needs to be provided by the user.

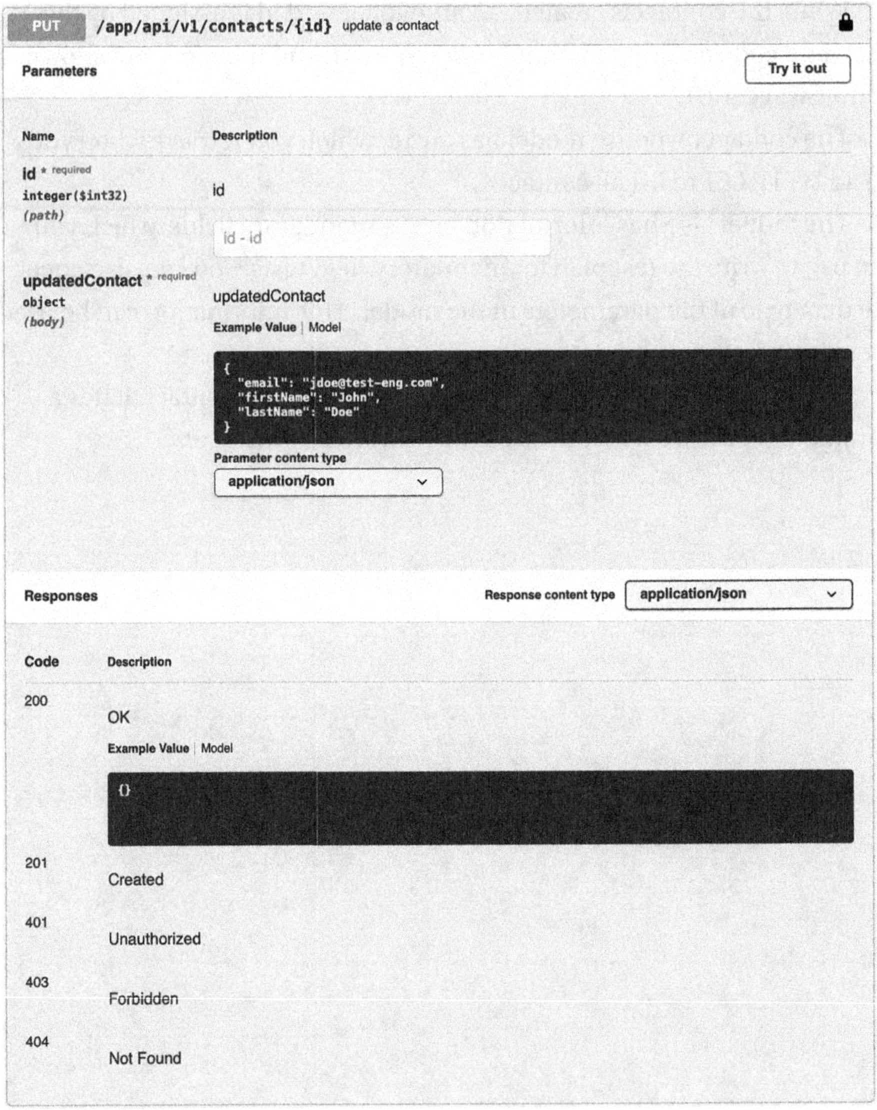

PUT	**/app/api/v1/contacts/{id}** update a contact	🔒

Parameters [Try it out]

Name	Description
id * required integer($int32) *(path)*	id [id - id]

updatedContact * required
object
(body)
	updatedContact
	
	Example Value | Model
	
	``
	{
	    "email": "jdoe@test-eng.com",
	    "firstName": "John",
	    "LastName": "Doe"
	}
	``
	
	Parameter content type
	[application/json ⌄]

Responses   Response content type [application/json ⌄]

Code	Description
200	OK Example Value | Model ``` {} ```
201	Created
401	Unauthorized
403	Forbidden
404	Not Found

Figure 11-7. *Swagger PUT request*

Swagger provides the id field. You can pass on the id and try the API, and it will work smoothly. You can copy the cURL command without any changes and execute it in the terminal window.

174

Let's try to find the contact; see Figure 11-8. You need to provide the contact id and the Swagger UI will show you the contact retrieved via the API. Check the response body shown in Figure 11-8.

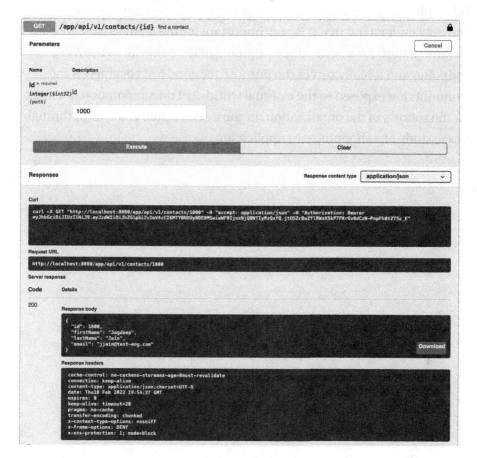

Figure 11-8. *Swagger GET request for finding a contact*

With this discussion, you have completed the Swagger overview. What you learned is that the API documentation provides the seed for the test plan and the tester can utilize it for writing API test plans. API documentation makes the tester's life much easier. Instead of guessing the response, they can now play around and understand the API behavior and perform effective test automation.

Summary

In this chapter, you learned about the need for API documentation. You explored the Swagger UI, which is used for API documentation. You now understand that it is very important for the team to have API documentation for a better understanding of the behavior of the API endpoint, and it really serves the purpose for good test coverage. If the endpoints are exposed to the external world, API documentation is a must for the success of the organization. In the next chapter, you will go through a case study of a shopping cart application.

CHAPTER 12

Case Study: Shopping Cart APIs

You covered API testing in the previous chapters. In this chapter, you will implement your new knowledge in a shopping cart project. You will learn how API testing is done in the software industry.

By the end of this chapter, you should be able to apply this knowledge to the projects you are assigned currently.

Appendix C has the details of deploying the shopping cart application that you are using for the case study.

One Klick Shop Inc.[1] is a pioneer in selling digital items online. They have a big team working 24/7, 365 days.

One Klick Shop Inc has evolved over a period of time and transformed from a monolithic architecture to a RESTful architecture. It has also adapted a JWT token-based authentication scheme for authenticating each user on its website.

Working on a new technology is a tough call in the online shopping industry. Timing is key since a delay of a few days in launching a new feature can give competitors a palpable competitive advantage. Even a small bug can cost much more than the overall budget of the project.

Let's find out in the following sections how testing of new APIs is completed by the development team.

---

[1] A hypothetical company used for case study discussion

Jay[2] has recently joined the development team as a SDET (Software Development Engineer in Test) and has been assigned the job of testing the new endpoints.

The new team is named NeuKode[3] and it is decided to do a three-week sprint cycle. CI/CD will be set up in the development and test environments, and the code will be deployed with every commit. The plan is to check at the end of the sprint when all looks green on CI/CD, and then the code will be deployed to the stage environment. After one week of testing on stage, it will be released to the production environment. The minimal viable product (MVP) is estimated to go to the market in 12 weeks, and the plan is to release the code base to production every month.

Feature List

The following is a list of features for the MVP:

1. New auth scheme (JWT token-based authentication)

2. User management CRUD operations

3. Authentication and authorization (user roles and permissions)

4. Address management (billing/shipping)

5. Payment details

6. Product catalog

7. Shopping cart

8. Order management

---

[2] A hypothetical name used for case study discussion
[3] A hypothetical name used for case study discussion

QA Responsibility Matrix

Let's create a fictional scenario to illustrate how this might work in real life. Jay is a senior team member. He asks for two team members who are proficient in Java, with one to three years of experience in software testing, or have good conceptual knowledge of software testing.

Jay informs his team that he has rich experience in writing test frameworks. He is an expert in Java and related technologies, and he will be the primary owner of the test framework code. One of his job roles will be to facilitate the testing engineers, thus making sure that everyone on the team is able to write the test scripts quickly and efficiently.

He conveys the responsibility matrix shown in Table 12-1 to the management.

Table 12-1. *Responsibility Matrix*

Experience Level	Responsibilities
0 to 1 year	• Write test scripts • Monitor test execution
1 to 5 years	• Includes above • Fix test script failures • Report bugs • Verify bugs • Document failures
6 to 10 years	• Includes above • Add code to the framework • Document usage • Test plan development • Test environment management • Debug production issues
10 years and above	• Includes above • Framework design • Code reviews • Participate in product roadmaps • Participate in product architecture discussion • Review design • POCs • Customer discussion

Now, let's take a look at the sprint cycle.

Sprint

The team agrees upon the sprint cycle and related activities detailed in Table 12-2.

Table 12-2. *Sprint Plan*

Sprint	Week #	Dev/Test/DevOps	Production Release
First	3	• Infra setup • Backlog grooming, story pointing, and sprint planning • Story grooming, development, and testing • Sprint demo • Backlog grooming, story pointing, and sprint planning • Deployment to stage/UAT	
Second	3	• Product management feedback, testing on stage environment • Story grooming, development, and testing • Sprint demo • Backlog grooming, story pointing, and sprint planning • Deployment to stage/UAT	**Production Deployment - Release I**

(continued)

Table 12-2. (*continued*)

Sprint	Week #	Dev/Test/DevOps	Production Release
Third	3	• Product management feedback, testing on stage environment • Story grooming, development, and testing • Sprint demo • Backlog grooming, story pointing, and sprint planning • Deployment to stage/UAT	**Production Deployment - Release II**
Hardening Sprint	3	• Product management feedback, testing on stage environment • Story grooming, development, and testing • Sprint demo • Backlog grooming, story pointing, and sprint planning • Deployment to stage/UAT • Bug fixes, regression testing, and sign off on stage/UAT environment	**Production Deployment - GA Release**

Based on this matrix, production deployment is set for every sprint. Now, let's explore how goal setting plays a crucial role in this process.

Goal Setting

Jay also sets up goals for himself, such as what activities and aspects need delegation to other engineering teams. These goals are additional goals, apart from the project goals. He discusses the goals with his manager and reaches an agreement on them.

1. With every sprint, he ask for the application performance report from the performance testing team.

2. At the start of every sprint, he gets in touch with the UX team to get a better understanding of the feature from the customer's point of view.

3. He improves the testing framework base code for extensibility to new projects.

4. He discuss the current progress with the product management/beta customers.

In addition to the above, he adds self-improvement goals for himself.

1. To improve the overall testing approach by sharing and learning the test process and activities, both within and outside the team

2. To write a blog every month based on the things he is doing

Sprint One

As a precursor to the sprint, the team has a quick huddle and they come up with the following items that will be used in all sprints.

Sprint Guidelines

The team agrees on the following items.

Definition of Done

The Development team finalizes the definition of done so that each deliverable is counted and finalized before it goes to production.

Jay takes these notes and pins them on his desk so that he remembers the definition while concluding the story/feature testing for the given sprint.

Story Pointing

The Development team also finalizes the story pointing method that they will be using for t-shirt sizing for pointing the stories.

Backlog Grooming

Scrum master Niel Knight[4] also facilitates the backlog grooming sessions' schedule. It is decided that at the end of each sprint, the team will gather for a discussion on the backlog for the next sprint. Product Manager Keith Strong[5] will host the meeting to discuss and prioritize the stories based on his discussion with beta customers and market research.

Neil Knight, the scrum master, also shares a dashboard that has various progress charts (such as sprint velocity). Jay bookmarks the chart that shows the current bugs' status. He remains updated with the number of bugs that are open/closed at any given point of time, and if there is anything that he can help with in closing the bugs.

---

[4] A hypothetical name used for case study discussion
[5] A hypothetical name used for case study discussion

Story Grooming

Keith Strong schedules the meeting for the stories that will be taken up in the sprint.

Jay goes through the stories and makes notes. This helps him in clarifying doubts during the meetings and also helping in undertaking effective testing.

QA Tasks

Jay starts a few of the things at the start of sprint #1. These are the items that will be required in the upcoming sprints.

Documentation

The very first thing he does is create a document named "OneKlickShop Testing" on Confluence[6], making sure that anyone joining the team has all the stuff at their disposal. Also, team members can refer to this document at any point during the product development or after.

He creates a few child pages under the main page.

The following is a list of the child pages with short descriptions:

1. Test Environment Setup - *IP/URL/SSH/proxy details*

2. Application Setup - *Required software installations and setup of required config*

3. Testing Objectives - *What the testing outcome should be*

4. CI/CD - *Jenkins URL and job details, plus information on the test execution cycle and test results*

---

[6]www.atlassian.com/software/confluence

5. Code Quality - *This will help in finding issues in the testing source code.*

6. Definition of Done - *This are agreed-upon points based on the team meeting for story closure.*

7. Test Framework Guide - *This document describes how to write an effective test script.*

8. Coding Guidelines - *This document describes how to write better test code.*

9. Code Review Guidelines - *Without putting in a lot of effort, these standard points help in quick test code reviews.*

10. Functional Testing - *Functional testing to be performed*

11. Non-Functional Testing – *Non-functional testing like security and performance testing*

12. Test Data - *How to get the testing data and the process of developing the test data for testing*

13. API Testing Guidelines - *These guidelines help in doing the effective testing without indulging too much in the story/feature*

14. UI Testing Guidelines - *These guidelines help in doing the effective testing without indulging too much in the story/feature*

15. Performance Testing Guidelines - *To be discussed with the product management*

16. Security Testing Guidelines - *To be discussed with the product management*

17.   Test Plans - *Central location of all test plans*

18.   Feature Delivery Timeline - *Includes JIRA stories with each release*

He makes a note to himself that the documentation should be updated all the time.

Test Environment

Jay starts working on setting up the testing infrastructure. He raises an IT request for a test VM for all testing needs. He lists all the required software development tools for setting up the application on the Confluence page.

Jay gets the test VM and starts setting up the testing environment.

Setting Up the Application

The Development team works in parallel and provides the initial commit to build the application. He follows the commands and starts setting up applications in the test environment.

QA Tools

Jay uses the following tools for test automation, test case management, and tester productivity.

Jenkins: `www.jenkins.io/download/` for test automation execution and finding regression in the application.

Testlink: `https://hub.docker.com/r/bitnami/testlink` for test case management. Testlink has various advantages over other test management tools, like you can create a test plan by selecting tests from test suites, you can assign a job to the QA, and there are various handy reports available. Also, tests can be exported to the work document.

Test execution has manual/automation options that help find out the automation coverage easily.

For tracking stories to test case relation, Jay uses a label in JIRA called `test_script` and plans to update JIRA once the story testing is completed. Also, the test cases are created in Testlink by the JIRA prefix, which helps to find the relevant test easily.

Requirements can be created in Testlink , which allows for traceability as well. It also conveys what tests were executed on which build. The tool has a good amount of information.

Jay knows that if SonarQube is set up, it is very easy to find code issues, if any. SonarQube checks the source code quality in terms of coding standards and Java concepts.

SonarQube: `www.sonarqube.org/downloads/` for test code quality check.

Jay sets up a code quality check tool. He sets up a SonarQube[7] docker container and adds the required configuration in the test framework `pom.xml`.

```
<plugin>
    <groupId>org.sonarsource.scanner.maven</groupId>
    <artifactId>sonar-maven-plugin</artifactId>
    <version>${sonar.version}</version>
</plugin>
```

After the installation of SonarQube with the help of the documentation on the SonarQube website[8], he tests the setup by scanning the project with the following command:

```
mvn sonar:sonar \
    -Dsonar.projectKey=eshop \
    -Dsonar.host.url=http://0.0.0.0:9000 \
    -Dsonar.login=<API_KEY>
```

---

[7] `www.sonarqube.org/`

[8] `https://docs.sonarqube.org/latest/setup/get-started-2-minutes/`

Continuous Integration/Continuous Deployment

CI/CD solves the infrastructure problem where it is not required to integrate and deploy the application source code manually. Nowadays it is an integral part of every software development team.

The Development team works in parallel to set up things in order to start working on the source code. They create a GitHub project for application development.

Jay also creates a test repository on GitHub, adds a project, and configures Jenkins with the GitHub repository. He also adds a configuration that allows the execution of tests with every commit in the GitHub repository. Without delay, he tests the Jenkins configuration so that there are no surprises in the next sprint.

The project manager asks Jay to push the testing project in the development repository and use the same dependencies in the testing project. Jay clarifies that the testing code is not a shippable product. Testers should not invest time in resolving the dependency. For example, if the development team is using some old version of Spring but the test framework requires a new version, then it will be a waste of time to make the test framework code backward compatible.

Targeted Features

Based on the feature list and product backlog, it is decided to develop the following features in the first sprint:

- New auth scheme (JWT token-based authentication)
- User management CRUD operations
- Authentication and authorization (user roles and permissions)

API Endpoints

The Development team provides the draft version of the Swagger document for the endpoints. Accordingly, Jay starts work on the test plan and the reference requirement document.

Unit Testing

Jay knows about the test pyramid. He asks the Development team for unit testing reports so that he knows the test coverage. Then he can work on the coverage of functional testing.

Jay sets up the test environment, and the test framework initial code is committed to the test repository. This is required to start writing test scripts.

Test Plan Development

Jay starts on the test plan based on the story discussion with the product manager and the story grooming meeting. He creates a test document and shares it with the team. The idea is to get early feedback, if any.

Jay has a quick meeting on the testing expectations and boundaries to make sure that he is not wasting time testing things that are not required at this point in the project, such as the risk associated with or without the redundant fields in the payload.

The approach is to complete the happy path first and then work on the exhaustive testing, if time permits in the sprint.

It is also discussed that requirements to test case traceability do not guarantee that the tests are not missing. It is a report to check whether the feature is completely missed by the tester or otherwise.

Based on various discussions, Jay creates the plan of the following things:

1. Story

2. Test summary

3. Precondition

4. Input value

5. Test execution steps

6. Expected result

7. Actual result

The test plan is located at https://github.com/Apress/Learn-API-Testing.

The test has data requirements. Jay starts working on the test data preparation in parallel with working on the test plan.

Test Data Preparation

In this sprint, the Development team targets to finish the user management CRUD API endpoints and implement authentication and authorization.

Jay creates test data using the test data generation tool available at www.mockaroo.com[9]. This is one of the best tools for generating API testing data. The free version is good enough, but the paid version is inexpensive.

Based on the test plan, he creates several payloads for testing the endpoints.

---

[9]www.mockaroo.com/

Manual Test Scripts

Jay sets up `www.testlink.org`[10] for test case management in sprint zero. He already created the project and now he adds the test cases from the spreadsheet to the Testlink project (after updating the spreadsheet format as per the Testlink requirements).

The test case has an automated field which he kept unchecked since he still has to work on the test automation scripts.

Postman

The development team provides the working API endpoints. Jay quickly sets up all the scenarios in Postman. This will help him to give quick feedback to the developers if they miss some scenarios.

He develops the Postman collections for high-level use cases and pushes them to the repository so that developers can pull the same and can run tests in their local environment.

He also shares the GitHub location with the team, `https://github.com/Apress/Learn-API-Testing`.

Test Automation

Jay completes the first round of testing using the Postman scripts and then he starts writing the test automation script.

He involves the other testing engineers to help him in writing the test scripts for the given API endpoints.

Jay puts up the guidelines for test automation scripts as per the categories listed in Table 12-3. He mentions to the team that they need to develop tests based on these categories.

---

[10] `www.testlink.org/`

Table 12-3. *Testing Categories*

JWT payload	User payload
	Admin payload
Admin	CRUD user
Authentication and authorization	Admin, user
User	Add, update, find billing details
	Add, update, find shipping details
	Add, update, find payment details
Response body	Actual vs. expected data
	Page, size
Schema validation	User schema
Error messages	User CRUD
Request headers	Supported type
	Response codes
Response body	Format unsupported
	Special characters
	Too long string
	Invalid method
	Invalid value
	Incorrect data type
	Empty data/payload
	Required fields
	Null
	Redundant fields
	Delete the deleted entity
	Duplicate check
	Limit/size/pagination/sorting

For JSON schema validation, Jay includes the hamcrest assert library on the UserSchemaTest class.

```
import static org.hamcrest.MatcherAssert.assertThat;
```

Here is the code snippet:

```
@Test(description = "verify user schema", priority = 1)
public void testUserSchema() {
 File file = new File(USER);
 request().get(OneKlickShop.FIND_USER.url(), query);

 assertThat(response().getResponse().getBody().asString(),
     matchesJsonSchema(file));
}
```

Jay and his team merge the code to the main branch after a code review meeting. Jay also updates the test plan column to the "Automated" flag based on the test script development, as per the test plan, in both the places: the spreadsheet and Testlink.

The code is located at https://github.com/Apress/Learn-API-Testing.

Test Suite

Jay creates a test suite named build-acceptance and adds the required TestNG XML file to the test repository. This test suite contains tests related to the feature in this sprint.

Parallel Test Execution

For faster test cycles, Jay configures the parallel test execution in the TestNg XML test suite file. He also verifies via jvisualvm[11] (a performance-monitoring tool for Java-based applications) shown in Figure 12-1 to check the thread count.

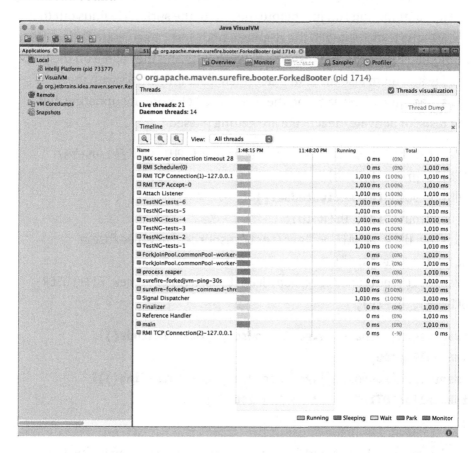

Figure 12-1. *Parallel tests*

---

[11] https://docs.oracle.com/javase/8/docs/technotes/tools/unix/jvisualvm.html

Test Execution

Jenkins is already configured on the test code GitHub repository. Jay schedules it to run every midnight on the latest development branch to find regressions, if any.

Alap[12], the other QA on the team, looks at the Jenkins build failures on the test automation run just before the end of the sprint. He finds out that a few of the tests related to the response body test category are failing. He immediately informs the respective developers and they agree on the bug.

Jay and team also find out that update user only works with the firstname and username, and the rest of the fields are not updating, but the tests for activate/deactivate are getting passed.

```
@Test(description = "verify response of PUT /api/v1/users/
{id}", priority = 4)
public void testActivateUser() {
 query.put("id", USER_ID);
 String USER_UPDATE = "src/test/resources/payload/user/
activateUser.json";
 request().put(OneKlickShop.UPDATE_USER.url(), new File(USER_
UPDATE), query);

assertThat(response().getResponse().getStatusCode()).
isEqualTo(200);
assertThat(response().getResponse().getStatusLine()).
isEqualTo("HTTP" + "/1" + ".1 200 ");
}
```

He reviews the test and finds out that the only assertion is checking the response status code. He creates a task to update the test script in the next sprint.

---

[12] Hypothetical name used for case study

Alap then reports the bug in the bug tracking system for triage since those bugs are not showstoppers; they will be added to the backlog for further prioritization.

Everyone in the team monitors the Jenkins test automation job. Jay now configures the Jenkins to send emails on the test failures.

Front-End Team

Since the APIs for authentication and authorization and user management are tested completely, Jay approaches the front-end team to make sure there are no issues in consuming the JWT token and the API they are consuming for UI development. He discussed the usage and issues, if any, with Sam[13], who is the QA on the front-end team. Sam conveys there are no issues on the API but says that the UI will also add error checks on the client side so that each request will go to the server only if it's a valid request. Jay makes a note and conveys to his team that the error handling is handled at the client side and is taken care of by the UI development team.

Sprint Nth

In the ongoing sprints, Jay follows the same routine of preparing the test plan, getting it reviewed by the team, adding tests to Testlink, developing Postman tests, and developing test automation scripts using RestAssured based on the categories he defined in sprint # 1. He also fixes the test script from the previous sprint and undertakes stage testing and release testing.

---

[13] Hypothetical name used for case study

Sprint Demo Feedback Testing

At the end of every sprint, the scrum master sets up the sprint demo meeting and the product management gives feedback to the development team. The product manager uses a stage environment for testing since it is a close replica of the production environment. Jay reports JIRA(s) and adds to the product backlog.

Jay incorporates the feedback in the test plan for further feature testing.

Hardening Sprint

Jay does the routine work in the hardening sprint. Also, he looks at the backlog of bugs. He schedules the bug triage meeting and finalizes on the list of bugs. These bugs are required to be fixed before the production release.

The Development team fixes all of the bugs and deploys the code to the staging environment after testing the development and test environments.

Sam, the QA from the UI team, also conveys that the UI is completed and deployed to the stage environment.

The next task for Jay and Sam is to do the release testing to make sure that the product goes live without the P0/P1 bugs.

Release Testing

The development and test environment have CI/CD set up and tests are executed with every commit. Now, since all of the features are developed and the required bugs are fixed, Jay, Sam, and the QA team complete the test script development. All tests are passed on to the development and test environments. The code is deployed to the stage environment. Jay and Sam run the test automation on the stage environment. They also perform ad-hoc smoke testing manually and certify the code to be moved to the production environment.

Jay and Sam give a nod to the production release and DevOps deploys the code to the production environment. Thereafter, Jay and Sam undertake the final round of smoke testing on the live environment. They created a test user and a dummy order. The **Production Deployment - GA Release** is completed and a release email is sent by the product manager to all stakeholders and beta customers.

After the production deployment, everyone in the team is very happy to see that the test automation has saved a lot of testing time by finding regression early in the development cycle.

Jay informs the external teams that the testing code is located in the GitHub repository located at `https://github.com/Apress/Learn-API-Testing`, and any input on the testing framework and source code is welcome for improving the same in the next project.

Summary

In this chapter, you learned about how to perform API testing in a software development project with the help of shopping cart APIs. You have learned about QA responsibility matrix, goal setting, sprint guidelines, QA tasks that involve documentation, test environment, CI/CD setup, test plan development, test data preparation, manual test scripts, importance of Postman while in feature testing, test automation and parallel test suite execution. You also learned how to do release testing at the end of the sprint. This chapter concludes API testing performed in the software industry.

APPENDIX A

Workstation Setup

This book has been written using macOS. It is expected that there will be no change in the command since we are using maven as the build and package management tool and Java as the programming language.

The following section has information on different environments on how to install the required software if not present on your workstation.

This book is based on JDK 8 and compatible Maven binary. Feel free to use the latest version of JDK with compatible Maven binary. For any issues, please report to the author or open an issue on the book's GitHub repository: https://github.com/Apress/Learn-API-Testing.

Java[1]

We are using Java as our language of choice for learning API testing.

The following section shows how to install Java on a workstation. After installation is completed, check the Java version using the following command. It should show JDK 8.

```
java -version
```

---

[1] Excerpt from: Sai Matam and Jagdeep Jain, *Pro Apache JMeter* (Apress, 2017)

MacOS

Download the Java Development Kit (JDK) from Oracle's website.

Pick JDK version 8. This is usually found on the web page by the name jdk-8...-macosx-x64.dmg.

Follow the instructions and complete the installation. To verify the installation of the Java runtime, run the following command in the terminal window:

```
$ java -version
```

Ubuntu

Open the terminal window in Ubuntu and issue the following command. It should show JDK 8.

```
$ sudo add-apt-repository ppa:openjdk-r/ppa
$ sudo apt-get update
$ sudo apt-get install openjdk-8-jdk
```

Linux

On Fedora, Oracle Linux, and Red Hat Enterprise Linux, open the terminal window and issue the following command:

```
$ su -c "yum install java-1.8.0-openjdk"
```

Windows

Download the Java Development Kit (JDK) from Oracle's website.

Pick JDK version 8 for Windows. This is usually found on the web page by the name jdk-8....-windows-x64.exe for 64-bit and jdk-8..windows-i586.exe for 32-bit. Depending on your machine configuration, download the required JDK.

Double-click the executable to launch the installer and follow the instructions.

Note   Set up JAVA_HOME if things are not working as expected.

Maven

This book instance is written using Maven 3.5.0, but any Maven which is compatible with JDK 8.0 can be used.

Maven can be installed via standard commands or downloaded manually from the Apache website `https://maven.apache.org/download.cgi` and installed on your workstation with the Maven executable set in the environmental path.

If Maven is installed manually, then we need to set `MAVEN_HOME` in the environment variable and add the bin directory in the path for Windows and the `PATH` variable on a Linux-based OS, so that we can execute Maven commands from any directory.

After installation, check the version; enter the following command in the terminal window:

```
$ mvn -version
```

MacOS

Maven can be installed using Homebrew. We can specify the Maven version to install. Refer to `https://formulae.brew.sh/formula/maven`.

```
$ brew install maven
```

Ubuntu

To install Maven, issue the following command in the terminal window:

```
$ sudo apt update
$ sudo apt install maven
```

Linux

To install cURL, enter the following command in the terminal window:

```
$ sudo yum install maven
```

Windows

For Windows, as of now there is no option to install Maven via executable. Unzip the binary and set the Maven executable path in the environment variables.

Maven Project

We are using Maven as our build and package management tool. Creating a Maven project takes less than a minute even though the Apache website says "Maven in 5 Minutes."[2]

Enter the following command in the terminal window:

```
$ mvn archetype:generate -DgroupId=com.apress.
app -DartifactId=app -DarchetypeArtifactId=maven-archetype-
quickstart -DarchetypeVersion=1.4 -DinteractiveMode=false
```

---

[2]https://maven.apache.org/guides/getting-started/maven-in-five-minutes.html

This will create a Maven project as an app.

```
$ cd app
```

And you can see the project details.

Or

Import as a Maven project into the IDE of your choice and check the directory structure. It should have /src/main and /src/test folders.

cURL

The following section shows how to install cURL on a workstation. After installation is completed, verify the installation using the following command. It should show various options of the cURL command.

```
curl -h
```

MacOS

To install cURL, enter the following command in the terminal window:

```
$ brew install curl
```

Ubuntu

To install cURL, enter the following command in the terminal window:

```
$ sudo apt-get install curl
```

Linux

To install cURL, enter the following command in the terminal window:

```
$ yum install curl
```

Windows

To install cURL, download the tool from the following URL: `https://curl.se/windows/`.

Postman

Download Postman from `www.postman.com/downloads/`.

IDE

Tests have been developed using IntelliJ. Another most popular IDE is Eclipse, and it can be used in a similar way. It is just that we need to import the project as a Maven project.

Tomcat

Download Tomcat binary from `https://tomcat.apache.org/download-90.cgi`.

MacOS/Ubuntu/Linux

Download Tomcat as a zip from `https://dlcdn.apache.org/tomcat/tomcat-9/v9.0.62/bin/apache-tomcat-9.0.62.tar.gz`.

Explode and put it in the /opt folder.

For unzipping and copying using a single command, enter the following command in the terminal window:

```
$ tar xvzf apache-tomcat-9.0.62.tar.gz -C /opt
```

From the Tomcat /bin directory, start the Tomcat server; enter the following command in the terminal window:

```
$ ./startup.sh
```

Windows

Download Tomcat as a zip from https://dlcdn.apache.org/tomcat/ tomcat-9/v9.0.62/bin/apache-tomcat-9.0.62-windows-x64.zip.

Create a folder in your home directory as tomcat/ and explode the zip file.

From the /bin folder you can start the Tomcat server.

APPENDIX B

Contact Management Application

The contact management application is a sample application that will be used to demonstrate API testing using cURL, Postman, and RestAssured.

Follow the below-mentioned instructions to run the contact management application in your local environment.

1. Clone the repository or download it as a zip from the GitHub location `https://github.com/apress/learn-api-testing`.

2. From the `Appendix-B/` directory, run the following command in the terminal:

   ```
   $ docker image build -t sa .
   ```

3. Once the image is ready, execute the below-mentioned command in the terminal window. This will start the contact management application.

   ```
   $ docker run -p 8080:8080 -t sa
   ```

These steps will start the application inside a docker container. This application has an in-memory HSQLDB as a database, so all the data will be wiped once the application shuts down or is stopped.

© Jagdeep Jain 2022
J. Jain, *Learn API Testing*, https://doi.org/10.1007/978-1-4842-8142-0

For the local Tomcat server, copy `app.war` from the `Appendix-B/` folder to the Tomcat `webapps/` folder and start the server using the environment-specific server start script.

Open the Postman application, enter the URL mentioned below, and provide the username and password in JSON format.

Application URL: `http://localhost:8080/app/auth/authenticate`

User credentials:

```
{

        "userName": "admin",
      "password": "test123"

}
```

Get the JWT from the `Headers` -> `Authorization` value column and use the same for the authentication to access the CRUD API calls.

Table B-1 shows the API endpoints of the contact management application.

Table B-1. *API Endpoints*

Add a contact	POST /api/v1/contacts
Update a contact	PUT /api/v1/contacts/{id}
Delete a contact	DELETE /api/v1/contacts/{id}
Find a contact	GET /api/v1/contacts/{id}
Get a list of all contacts	GET /api/v1/contacts

The sample payload for adding and updating a contact is as follows:

```
{

        "firstName": "Jagdeep",
        "lastName": "Jain",
        "email": "jj@learn-api-testing.com"

}
```

Swagger

Once the contact management application has started, open the URL
`http://localhost:8080/app/swagger-ui/` in the browser to check
the API documentation of the contact management application in the
Swagger UI.

APPENDIX C

Shopping Cart Application

The shopping cart application is an online shopping application that will be used to demonstrate API testing for a case study using RestAssured.

Follow the below-mentioned instructions to run the shopping cart application in your local environment.

1. Clone the repository or download it as a zip from the GitHub location `https://github.com/apress/learn-api-testing`.

2. From the `Appendix-C/` directory, run the following command in the terminal:

   ```
   $ docker image build -t sa .
   ```

3. Once the image is ready, execute the below-mentioned command in the terminal window. This will start the shopping cart application.

   ```
   $ docker run -p 8080:8080 -t sa
   ```

These steps will start the application inside a docker container. This application has an in-memory HSQLDB as a database, so all the data will be wiped once the application is shut down or stopped.

© Jagdeep Jain 2022
J. Jain, *Learn API Testing*, https://doi.org/10.1007/978-1-4842-8142-0

For the local Tomcat server, copy `eshop.war` from the `Appendix-C/` folder to the Tomcat `webapps/` folder and start the server using the environment-specific server start script.

Open the Postman application, enter the URL mentioned below, and provide the username and password in JSON format.

Application URL: `http://localhost:8080/eshop/login`

```
User credentials
{
    "username": "admin@oneklickshop.com",
    "password": "test123"
}
```

Get the JWT from the response and use the same for the authentication to access API calls.

Swagger

Once the shopping cart application has started, open the URL `http://localhost:8080/eshop/swagger-ui/` in the browser to check the API documentation of the shopping cart application in the Swagger UI.

Index

A

Agile development, 12, 166
Amazon mobile app, 166
API-based software
 applications, 25, 29
API development, 9, 87, 165
API documentation, 165, 175
 development artifacts, 166
 standard, 166
 using Swagger (*see* Swagger)
API endpoints, 123, 129, 139, 150,
 165, 167, 190
API test coverage, 85, 104
API testing, 3
 advantages, 8
 API testing paradigm, 81
 authentications, 31
 back end/middle tier, 5
 business workflows, 3
 CDCT, 92
 GUI *vs*. API test development, 8
 header testing (*see* Header
  testing)
 HTTP(S), 4
 internal *vs*. external APIs, 92, 93
 Klick Shop Inc., 177
 negative testing, 92, 93

 request body (*see*
  Request body)
 request methods, 4
 response body, 91
 ROI, 5
 schema validation, 82–85
 test coverage, 85
 test framework (*see* Test
  framework, API testing)
 test plan, 4
 test scripts, 82
 tools, 4
 types, 6
 use cases, 82
 workflows, 82
API testing paradigm, 81, 165
Application programming
 interfaces (APIs), 1
 in middle tier, 2
 service-based model, 2
 testing (*see* API testing)
 typical service-based software
  application architecture, 2
 typical web application, 2, 3
Assertj, 73, 108, 120, 123, 125
Assertj 3.9.1, 125
Authentication endpoint, 43

© Jagdeep Jain 2022
J. Jain, *Learn API Testing*, https://doi.org/10.1007/978-1-4842-8142-0

U, V

W

X, Y, Z

Printed in the United States
by Baker & Taylor Publisher Services